Darkling's Beasts and Brews

Poetry with a Drink on the Side

LVP
PUBLICATIONS

Edited by Darkling, Lycan Valley's Horror Host
Cover Design by Kealan Patrick Burke
Darkling Art by M Wayne Miller, Copyright © 2018 LVP Publications
Clown Art by Stephen Cooney, Copyright © 2018 LVP Publications

Darkling's Beasts and Brews Copyright © 2018 LVP Publications
Poetry Copyright © 2018 Individual Authors
Recipes Copyright © 2018 Darkling and LVP Publications

Printed in the United States of America

Lycan Valley Press Publications
1625 E 72nd St STE 700 PMB 132
Tacoma, Washington 98404 United States of America

First Printing

ISBN: 0-9987489-5-1
ISBN 13: 9780998748955

Hey, all you Beasties and Ghouls, Darkling here.

Welcome to the Machleif Cemetery—where the dead don't care and the living don't dare. Usually.

Tonight we're opening the blood gates for a good old fashioned graveyard party. Everyone's invited so bring your friends, bring your enemies, bring your deceased. We don't discriminate just because some of you have breath and some smell like death.

I'll be your graveyard host for the night, and I've got a special treat for those of you who like your scares with a bit of flow. Within these pages, you'll find terrifying verses, supernatural sonnets, and dreadful odes for your voracious literary appetites—all extraordinary tales told in sinuous verse. Some long, some short, but all chilling. For those of you who like it short—but never sweet—I've even thrown in some shots of Haiku...

Speaking of shots, did y'all think this was just another book of spooky poetry and deadly lyrical compositions? You couldn't be more wrong. Every tale (or tail) included comes paired with a special drink recipe straight out of my own personal recipe box—some extremely spirited and some more restrained—each one crafted to tickle your taste buds.

You'll find a complete reference guide for navigating your way through this party at the end of book, but here's a quick tip to help you get started: the Coffee & Tea, Milkshakes and Party Punch sections contain both alcohol and non-alcohol recipes. Drinks containing alcohol are listed first in each section.

Cocktails & Mixed Drinks and Haiku Shots all contain alcohol and you'll find only non-alcohol drinks in the Smoothie and Bonus Clown sections.

I hope you find them all deliciously palatable. But do remember to imbibe conscientiously.

While no one likes an overly intoxicated nuisance, some of the less human guests do fancy a marinated snack. And if y'all haven't been on this planet for enough trips around the sun to guzzle legally, we suggest that you forego doing so.

We do love your company here at the Machleif Cemetery, but we prefer y'all come of your own volition and not in a coffin. Now that all the boring stuff is out of the way, go have a drink, read the poem and enjoy the party.

I gotta run y'all... the Spirits of the Damned await!

Love and Horror,
Darkling

COFFEE AND TEA

Coffee isn't just for mornings around here. When you're dead, it's always time for a caffeine boost. And tea—hot or cold—is good any time. Don't just take my word on it. Ask the Mad Hatter. He'll tell ya. He may even drop by for a cup or two.

For all you Beasties and Ghouls out there whose blood runs a little cold, these recipes are sure to heat things up a bit, get the circulation moving.

You'll find recipes here with alcohol listed first and non-alcoholic drinks to follow. But hey, if y'all want to ditch the alcohol, these recipes are simple enough to leave it out. Of course, if y'all want to spike the rest, just slip in a bit of vodka.

Enjoy, y'all!

The Drinks

Monster Mash

Red Velvet Morning

Full Moon Transformation

Chocolate Amaretto Wendigo

Butterscotch Night Owl

Enchanted Faerie

Black Dog Mocha

Vampire and Cream Macchiato

Sweet & Spicy Werewolf Mocha

Wendigo Pumpkin Pie

Cinnamon Ginger Gargoyle

Undead Blackberry Brandy

Redcap Zinger

Whispering Moonlight Tea

Lost Princess

Iced Brazilian Cha Mate

Scottish Kelpie Secret Tea

Luring Temptation Tea

Wild Werewolf Chai

Strawberry Rooibos Soul Eater

Chimera Freedom Green Tea

The Poetry

The Monster Mash by John C Mannone

The Morning Named Apollo: A Chimeric Blood Song by Stephanie Wytovich

The Lycanthrope by Paula Berman

The Hunter by EM Eastick

The Eyes by Mark Mihalko

Fated to Die by Sara Tantlinger

With Bared Teeth by Javier Gomez

In Our Past Mortality by Jay Rohr

Lust in the Full Moon by Khalil Goddard

Frontier Winter by CJ Thompson

Evolution of a Young Lover by Frank Heather

Nosferatu by Michael H Hanson

Redcap by Kurt Newton

The Night Whispers by Sarah Cannavo

Monster Mash

Get It

8 oz Eggnog
2 oz White Coffee Espresso
3 oz Irish Cream Liqueur
1 oz Vodka
Cinnamon

Mix It

1. Brew white coffee espresso, add vodka and set aside to cool.
2. In tall glass, mix egg nog and irish cream.
3. Fold (or mash) in coffee/vodka, sprinkle with cinnamon and enjoy!

Read It

Who doesn't love a good party? Well, plenty of people, obviously. But all you Beasties and Ghouls look ready to party, so let's open the doors and bring these monsters in! Y'all better mix this up and grab your drink before they do! They brought their own too, but these monsters sure do look thirsty...

The Monster Mash

They all gathered—
zombies, vampires, and werewolves;
banshees, wendigos, and witches;
hellhounds and goblins;
fairies, haunts and trolls;
shape shifters and invisible beings
—they all came to the BYOB party,
it was a monster mash.

And so they staggered
through the oaken doors—stoned
castle on the hill—wearing their favorite
human costume,
but anyone could tell by what they drank
who they really were
beneath their Halloween disguises.
Some such as these:

Dead Man's Drink
Bile on the rocks
Pinch of zombie bitters
(for hung-over heads)

Bloody Marie
Mulled with celery & cilantro
Inside a Dracula cup
(but no garlic-salted rim)

Hairy Navel
Southern peach, sliced
Soaked in wolf bane & brandy
(Drink under full moon)

Spirit ethers
Thin air
Lemon twist
Invisible Drink

When the belfry clock clanged
the midnight hour, they all flew out like bats
out of hell, clawed their makeshift skins off,
making delirious sounds
as they embarked for spirits
of the valley—the hunting
and haunting
of humans had begun.

~ John C Mannone
Tennessee, USA

Red Velvet Morning

Get It

8 oz Whole Milk

4 oz Half-and-Half

¼ tsp Vanilla Extract

¼ tsp Macadamia Nut Syrup

1 Tbsp Red Velvet Syrup

1 ½ oz White Chocolate Liqueur

3 oz Espresso

Whipped Cream for topping

Mix It

1. Steam milk and half-and-half or gently heat over low heat.
2. Add vanilla, syrups and white chocolate. Add espresso.
3. Pour into mug and top with whipped cream.

Read It

If you're lucky, there's a morning after for every day. Some days you're well-rested and some days—well, some days you're reborn into something wicked. We all have mornings like that. So, grab a Red Velvet and prepare for A New Awakening...

The Morning Named Apollo:

A Chimeric Blood Song

Here, in the awakening,
Apollo wraps the Chimera warm
in lunacy, an embrace she holds
until the sun crests over the brimstone sky,
the scent of her forefathers' rage
a welcome plume as she rises, a goddess of trinity,
to swallow fire and bathe in the bone dirt
of her species.

Her den, a now savage haven, collects the
whispers of blood-colored ruins, her heart beat
a constant reminder of the poison trap
ticking toxic inside her, a forever clock
counting down to her extinction,
one slaughter at a time.

Yet a servant to the darkness, a thrice-hybrid shadow,
she stalks the tunnels in mourning, an ancient ritual
against the roadmap of slavery, this, her new morning feed:
the serpent eats the goat, the lion roars,
an elemental digestion, this monstrous rebirth,
she conquers the venom by ingesting it,
enters a new womb of demon:
this feral toxicity, this untamed hunger
she'll kill the sun, feast on the gods,
claim the sky in the name of Chimera,

A new awakening.

A new world order.

~ Stephanie Wytovich
Pennsylvania, USA

Full Moon Transformation

Get It

2 oz Kahlúa®
1 Tbsp Vanilla Syrup
2 tsp Instant Coffee Granules
12 oz Black Cherry Soda

Mix It

1. Add instant cofee to the bottom of a tall glass. Layer Kahlúa® and syrup.
2. Slowly fill the glass with cold black cherry soda.
3. Stir gently as mixture will foam.

Read It

Ever been out on a date with a guy when he suddenly takes off his clothes and turns into a hairy beast? I don't know about you but a night out surrounded by romantic moonlight, a gorgeous lake, and an unforgettable transformation sounds like a dream date to me...

The Lycanthrope

I loved him so hard there was no room in my heart to spare
For any other feelings when he took me
Out to the lake that night. Through the canopy of trees,
The full moon illuminated the planes of his face
I thought, *finally!* when he pulled his shirt over his head
Oh for the courage to trace the line of his clavicle,

His breastbone, to caress his chest—
But I didn't dare.

Unbuckled his belt, then the leather swish
The musical jangle as his jeans hit the ground
And his body was bared
To me. So great was my desire
That I felt no panic when he, bathed in moonlight,
Split his false skin, shucked it off and
Showed me who he really was.

I didn't even scream
At the sight of his full glory.
My flesh between his teeth
Sang hallelujah
and then
he made a monster
of me.

~ Paula Berman
New York, USA

Chocolate Amaretto Wendigo

Get It

1 square Dark Chocolate

8 oz Brewed Coffee

1 ½ oz Amaretto Liqueur

Mix It

1. Place chocolate in bottom of mug.
2. Add hot, freshly brewed coffee.
3. Top with amaretto.

Read It

Alright all you Beasties and Ghouls, y'all know how the saying goes. Be careful what you hunt for, you just might get it. Or maybe you'll find something much, much worse. I wouldn't want to meet this monster in the dark, dark woods. Or anywhere, for that matter. Humans never learn...

The Hunter

Cedar stands, basaltic cliffs, an isolated Eden.
Bracken ferns and fiddleheads, trampled down and eaten.
Tinder flashed and flared to life. The hunter watched the flames.
And waited for the Wildman who went by many names.

Timber crackled, branches fell, fire across his chest.
A gangly figure through the smoke, ten foot tall, no less.
Shotgun blast, the hunter screams, the creature bending low,
Hungry eyes and razor teeth, not Bigfoot—Wendigo.

~ EM Eastick
Colorado, USA

Butterscotch Night Owl

Get It

16 oz Brewed Coffee
1 oz Butterscotch Sauce
1 oz Dark Brown Sugar
¼ tsp Pure Vanilla Extract
2 oz Heavy Cream, room
    temperature

Mix It

1. Add butterscotch sauce, brown sugar and vanilla to a mug; mix well.
2. Pour hot brewed coffee and stir.
3. Gently pour cream over hot coffee.

Read It

The eyes are the windows to the soul. Oh, who am I kidding? That line's been done to death. And believe me, I know death. Even so, there are some windows you just shouldn't peek into no matter how clear the view...

The Eyes

In the darkness it waited
Two bright eyes shadowed within a veil
A lone heart tucked away
Tonight was not the night to show the true self
Not the night to show the depths of the withering souls lost
There were things more important than the spirits

In silence, it waited for the evening to come
The smoke clung to every particle of air
The stale atmosphere and dim light set the perfect mood
The eyes watched from the corner where no light could see
Where no vision would survive

The eyes were not worthy of the glow
Not worthy of the pure caress held in the hands
The dull sound of a footfall echoed through the bar
The eyes quivered with excitement
The pain may finally end

Through the haze, the eyes caught a glimpse of an angel
A dark and foreboding apparition of light
Petrified, it could not move from this shallow grove of darkness
It could not confirm the suspicion that the end was at hand

The eyes again scanned the alley
No souls, no spirits, no angels
Alone again, staring into oblivion
Nothing was visible; nothing was near
Only the faint glimmer of forbidden brightness lay on the horizon
An unholy resting place for the demons of the darkness
Alone no more

A soft thud echoed through the misty street
The two yellow eyes could not hide anymore
The time was near

The radiance watched with a cruel intensity
Perfect warmth for this placid night
An invisible grin drawing it closer
Comforting the shivering flesh
The dense smoke, the dying lights, the tears of anguish

One tortured soul indifferent about the future

Two eyes penetrating the passion

Awaiting its sentence

Again, the eyes grew wide

Drawing a deep breath to muster all the courage

All the vile obscurity that controlled its heart

A fitting end to a torturous existence

The flickering cone called

The flame igniting the scarred tissue

The eyes were not meant for this moment

Not prepared to face an evil eternity

Timid and scared beyond comprehension

The eyes closed as it crept forward

Blinding itself from the essence that lay ahead

Another being moved in tandem

Trudging closer to Dante's forbidden realm

Its presence soothing the fears captured beneath the eyes

Slicing through the fog with a dagger of despair

Tearing at the blood that filled its void

Alive no more, the eyes could see the river of unshed tears

The darkness in the light

~ Mark Mihalko
Pennsylvania, USA

Enchanted Faerie

Get It

16 oz Double-strength Brewed
Coffee
1 oz Habanero Honey
2 oz Half-and-Half

Mix It

1. Brew coffee double strength.
2. Add honey and dissolve.
3. Top with half-and-half.

Read It

Free will or fate? Hmm, does it really make any difference in the end? I mean, y'all know the end result is the same right? Ah, well, the habenero honey and half-and-half will make purgatory sting a little less and even add a little shimmer to your pretty skin...

Fated to Die

I am illusory
citrus-flavored and fluttering
prophesizing how winter
tastes like dirt-scented fatality
as the Faerie Queen warns
do not confuse fay with fey—
meaning fated to die
like October, like leaves, like love,

But I already hold so much death
within the blink of my eyes
minty green irises sharp as grass blades
because this is the enchantment of fairies
flying into your life on ragwort stems
on the backs of blue jays
on the whisper of the devil
blowing through the trees,

Saying pay your tithe to Hell
my winged children,
but say your prayers to Heaven
because no one knows if fairies
were banished by God
or not dark enough for Satan,

But purgatory on Earth
doesn't seem too bad
as we make our homes between curves
of vines, sleep within diamond dewdrops
make love on flower petals
feast on blackberries and acorns

Just do not mistake blood
for the sheen of glitter on wings
despite the way it shimmers
on your pretty skin,
no matter how many times
you bathe the ethereal glow
of your sprite juices

You cannot evade
death's oncoming demand,
cannot use your ragged wings to escape
the snake in Paradise's garden.

~ Sara Tantlinger
Pennsylvania, USA

Black Dog Mocha

Get It

8 oz Strong Brewed Coffee
4 oz Dark Chocolate Chips
2 oz Chocolate Milk
1 Tbsp Caramel Syrup

Mix It

1. Add chocolate chips to the bottom of a large mug.
2. Pour hot coffee over chocolate; stir until chocolate is melted.
3. Add chocolate milk and top with caramel syrup.

Read It

Y'all know chocolate is toxic to dogs, right? Seriously, don't give this to the family pet. Not even a lick. On the other hand, if y'all find yourself in a situation where ya need to stop the black dog's deadly path, this might do the trick...

With Bared Teeth

A sombre tale here I recall
from North of Albion fair and proud
where clouds and rain rule o'er all
and o'er all gales sing aloud.

There was a beast that prowled the night,
a fiend so black as soot made ink,
a more grim and unholy sight
than any mind would dare to think.

At dusk in York the curtains fell,
in every house were sashes nailed,
and the whole town had not a soul
that dared to tread the demon's trail.

Thus came a man in Whitby born,
a stranger brought by tales of woe,
a fearless scholar of The Golden Dawn
who vowed to deal a fatal blow.

In a damp grey gorge he made the call
through arcane signs from long ago.
The hound's howl shattered the thrall,
a piercing sound from the foul foe.

Beast and man all night they fought
with tooth and nail, and staff and sword
'til the mage fell and then he thought
that was his chance to use the word.

A mystic cipher known by him alone
which stopped the black dog's deadly path
and moved his soul from flesh and bone
into the hellhound filled with wrath.

There lied the corpse in Troller's Gill
of a brave warlock who prevailed
against an eldritch evil on a forlorn hill
to claim a victory that no one hailed.

For the barghest lived forevermore
with hero's mind in monstrous cage
of rending claws, of bark and roar,
haunting the groves and now the page.

~ Javier Gomez
Lancashire, UK

Vampire and Cream Macchiato

Get It

12 oz Strong Brewed Coffee
1 oz Vanilla Syrup
$\frac{1}{2}$ oz Raspberry Syrup
2 oz Half-and-Half
Fresh Raspberries

Mix It

1. Add vanilla and raspberry syrup to strong brewed coffee.
2. Pour in lightly steamed or room temperature half-and-half.
3. Top with whipped cream and fresh raspberries.

Read It

This is a drink and a poem after my own heart. If had a heart, that is. After all, I am dead and well, nevermind. Even blood drinking corpses can appreciate the beauty and sweetness of fresh raspberries and cream. And, unlike me, this poem puts it into tremendously beautiful words...

In Our Past Mortality

Admiring a moon dog
I asked a ghost in the fog
If the gala in Prague
Was the epilogue,
The last celebration
Of a shadow congregation,
A final bit of glitz and glamour
Before the fall of a hammer
Driving the point home
There's no more shine on the chrome.

And I realize I've been a camera
Passively recording living anaphora,
Gilded memories made phrases
Repeated to feed the blazes
Lighting the long road thru
The dark blue
Where I met Carmilla, Ruthven,
And a Byronic coven.

Our collective aspiration
To enjoy damnation.
Finding ourselves villains who seemed
No better than those who deemed
Us vile, we reveled in being loathed
By hypocrites whose hate exposed
A desire to be as free as we.
Nowhere was this easier to see
Than Weimar Germany.

Reckless nights in Berlin,
Cabarets fit for Cain
Permitting every sin.
Unrolling red ribbons
From—I couldn't begin
To remember them:
Rosie, Helga, Frenchie, Fritz, *und* Lulu
Just to name a few.
Pleasant dreams of blood and thunder
Feeding myriad forms of hunger.
Willkommens-Sünde
Keine Notwendigkeit für alle Gründe.

But never inclined to torch rallies
We departed for Appalachian valleys,
And Faulknerian topographies
Wherein our biographies
Would have to attest
We felt better there—blessed.
The molasses flow of Southern insanity
Made hedonism seem rife with banality.
Torn by the cascade of subtle blades
Families decayed over decades.
We watched the great rise and fall,
Sometimes without our assistance at all.
Yet, being paragons of frankness
There soon seemed a certain sameness
To these caged wild hearts—
Ends foreseeable regardless of starts;
And though the Southern gothic connected
It all so slowly infected.
Our *belle rêve* permitted tragedy
To close the century,
The death of our common union
Leading to dispersal and disillusion.

We are, but blood drinking corpses
Whose course is
Spelled out in fang scars like Braille
Instructing each coffin nail.

So alone I drifted to New Orleans,
Where I met the finest of Creole queens.
She harvested the sweat of the sun
To pay for hurricanes
So *tempête et stress* was never done.
She returned my tongue
To the taste of fun.
Ever youthful, I watched how she aged.
In all that brief time, her life never seemed staged.
With her underground
I thought of us as Cemetery and Sundown,
Haunting her grave
Until the loss inspired me to crave
Old company. In the hope time mends
I sought my lost friends.

But we can't be what we were

Without daring to incur

The risk of putrefying

In a past undying.

Our history is the portal

Through which we lick being mortal.

Yet as the epilogue closes

I smell the attar of roses.

A second volume begins

For my wheel ever spins.

~ Jay Rohr
Illinois, USA

Sweet and Spicy Werewolf Mocha

Get It

4 oz Half-and-Half

4 oz Evaporated Milk

1 ½ Tbsp Cocoa Powder

2 Tbsp Raw Sugar

¼ tsp Ground Cinnamon

½ tsp Pure Vanilla Extract

⅛ tsp Pure Almond Extract

2 shots Espresso

Ground Cloves

Mix It

1. Heat half-and-half and evaporated milk in a heavy saucepan over medium heat.

2. Whisk cocoa powder, sugar and cinnamon into milk mixture until frothy and slightly thickened. Stir in vanilla and almond extracts.

3. Pour into cup and add espresso. Sprinkle with cloves.

Read It

Walking home alone at night is never a good idea. Walking home alone on the night of a full moon is fatal. If y'all are going to do it anyway, bring along this sweet and spicy mocha and don't say I didn't warn ya...

Lust in the Full Moon

Lady Selene shows her white face
against the backdrop of luxuriant night
she casts her smiling light down
upon the darkened land
peace rules for the slumbering
yet those who hunt and hide
in the time before the sun comes again
are this night in hiding, in fear
for terror is unleashed by sweet Selene
though she sanctions not this beast.

Stalking the places on the edge of sanity
the man-beast hides his metamorphosis
as teeth grow, fur sprouts, eyes yellow
and the howls of hell break out
the werewolf runs seeking prey
there will be death this night
the creatures of nature know and hide

but man, nature's enemy
knows not the doom that approaches
though that doom seeks their flesh.

Death comes from within their fallen race
a species hybrid of Satan's creation
slavering, hungering, blind instinct
leads the beast to seek his prey
little more than a child
she walks alone on lonely road
a shortcut to take her swiftly home
instincts dulled by luscious wine
and a night of thrilling, lustful pleasure
the man-wolf breathes in her sin.

He comes at her swiftly from behind
jaws dripping, eyes glowing
with unhuman lust and greed
driving him insanely on
his time is forever now
'neath cloudless naked skies
she screams once as his teeth rend flesh
from a throat so white
exposed to his greedy lustful gaze
and his howl wakes the dead.

Tainted blood pounds through his body

swelling the musculature of evil

her blood fresh and appetising

alcohol adding a sweet piquancy

that fires the desires deep within

his hands take hold more gently

as her blood spurts into his insatiable maw

her life is his life now

though his lust is only part slaked

more victims will fall tonight.

~ Khalil Goddard
London England

Wendigo Pumpkin Pie

Get It

2 shots Espresso
1 cup Whole Milk
1 Tbsp Pure Pumpkin Puree
1 Tbsp Raw Sugar
Pinch of each: Cinnamon,
    Allspice, Ginger, Cloves
¼ tsp Pure Vanilla Extract
¼ tsp Pure Almond Extract
Whipped Cream

Mix It

1. Combine milk, pumpkin puree, sugar and spices in a saucepan and heat over medium heat.
2. Add vanilla and almond extracts; whisk until frothy.
3. Pour mixture over espresso in a large mug. Top with whipped cream.

Read It

Mmmm...there's nothing better than warm pumpkin pie on a cold winter night. It's a perfect mix for a chilly night, whether you're following tracks under a snow-clotted sky or curled up beneath the boughs of a pine...

Frontier Winter

1. NIGHT

The hills took our brother.
He went to check lines on the northern slopes,
and didn't come back.
Snow fell for three days after he left.
When we went looking, a blanket of white buried his tracks.
Nothing moved under the trees while we called his name.
Nothing moved, and nothing moved.

Whenever we turned our heads to look, the snow and trees and shade
went still again.
We left when the wind rose and sunset reddened the hills.
We found no trace of our brother.

We all speak less, with our brother gone.
But in the evenings, with the weight of a nearly-silent day on our shoulders,
we'll circle around the stove.
In the bright flickering glow,
one of us starts to sing.

The sound of us washes out
into the vast, chilly night.
It doesn't fill the emptiness.
But the singing makes a shape in the silence,
bearing up the oceans-weight of it,
so we draw chilly breaths for another day,
so we can pour ourselves out into music
in the dark of another night.

We started losing animals from our snares.
We thought for a few days it might be our brother.
Then we found the raw red remnants in the snow.
No hunger of his ever did that.

We'd laid by enough food to see us through without the traps.
But we stopped going out alone.
We check the lines near the house,
and hope that come spring the beast moves on.

We sang again last night,
and this morning I found tracks in the snow
in front of the house.
I do not think it is afraid.

♏. SLEEP

We are thick with the songs of crickets and whip-poor-wills.
The air too heavy
to sleep with windows closed.
Some nights, the wind brings a high, thin howling down from the peaks.

We fish and cure, forage and dry, sow and reap,
Never in groups of less than three.
We go further into the hills
While the lights lie long
But we are always back by dark.

I dream all through the shortened nights.
I dream
That I followed my brother out into the storm,
Tracked his prints as they filled with snow,
as the chill seeped up my legs and settled in my chest.
I inhaled, letting my ribcage bloom with cold, and kept walking.

I walked and walked, over ground brighter than the snow-clotted sky.
I followed his tracks to a narrow gorge, high in the hills.
I heard his voice
thrown back to me on the wind.

I could not siphon fear from excitement in that sound.
I tried running, but the wash of snow against my thighs slowed me.
The cold air ran ragged in my lungs.
Still, I pushed upslope, trying to catch sight of him.
The walls of the gorge rose around me,
and his footprints spread out further and further,
As though he'd grown impossibly tall
or been lifted up into the air.
I followed, until I could not find the next.
The snow fell patiently.
I would not make it home.
I crawled beneath the boughs of a pine
and slept.

M. DREAM

I dreamt the tides changed in my veins,
That cold rooted in my chest
So my breath no longer steamed in the air,
And stars lit the snow like day.
I opened my mouth,
Wind howled when I tried to sing.
I turned down valley,
My family's house blazed,

A sun set on the valley floor,
Bright with harmony
And warm.
I turned to run,
My feet skimming over the snow,
Lighter and lighter,
Until I moved like wind,
Like nothingness
Between the trees.

I crouched in the snow,
Nearly blind with the light of them.
Again, wind howled
When I tried to sing.
I left my name for them
Etched with fingers sharp and strong
In the wood
Of the door.

I do not know
If they will dream
Of me.

~ CJ Thompson
Massachusetts, USA

Cinnamon Ginger Gargoyle

Get It

4 Tbsp Coffee Grounds
⅛ tsp Cinnamon
⅛ tsp Ginger
⅛ tsp Cardamom
1 Tbsp Orange peel
1 Tbsp Sweetened Condensed
    Milk

Mix It

1. Mix coffee grounds, spices and orange peel in a small bowl.
2. Brew mixture in a french press or steep in boiling water for 5 minutes.
3. Pour into mug and stir in sweetened condensed milk.

Read It

Poor Onigawara. Even gargoyles need love, right? A nice cup of hot coffee with a little cinnamon and ginger ought to do the trick. It'll warm up the coldest of hearts, even this stone cold lover...

Evolution of a Young Lover

I.

There is no such canopy as the one
I was promised in her arousing love.

II

This is the night of the gargoyle whose fog floats like a sinusoidal wave
in the pelvic wind, puddlemud spraying everywhere.

The night when their cactus seeds and mauvish debaucheries crack open:
gargoyles drinking like weird caitiffs vomiting on this diatomaceous earth.

Theirs is the night of staring at zoo-animal-strangers
pressing their faces against glass cages cement floors.

The blades of grass have dropped dead—no greenery
on the grey, yellowed over with cancerous warts
erupting like soufflés: like uncoiled rancid oil,
flooding the streets with a new breed of green.

Strange men dig up the crumbling buildings
stinking of weak graphite, fortified in appearance
despite the cicadas who reappear to haunt the sky's diminishing ramparts

And the veneer of stars falls away—yes, wilting
above a fruitful evening of drunken varmint laughter.

Throngs of pale lunatics pace Manhattan
in tempestuous motion
about the axis of the horizon,
nothing resting and nothing coming to rest.

♏

She became heavier than a simplicity to me,
much more capable than a pretty jointure of mouths,
distant like the other end of a taut string
galvanized by a harsh current.

Wrestling in the fray, she quit to laugh.
Laughing, she learned to summon herself.
And summoning herself, she lost everything
and stranded her own bones in a slanted territory of pain

Her cavern of terror grew dark
like the rot at the center of our ghoulish love.

IV

Everyone is drunk.
I feel cruel.

As long as there is night
there are demons
and justice is knowing
when to ask them to tilt the scale.
This is my expertise.

Breathing down my neck,
the sky's vastness once intimidates me as I loom and lurch
my stony brow and flatter the stasis so the sky may tilt.

How came it to be that her kisses of mine
landed on that lean superlative sexing up her eyes?

It all brings me back to the pinnacle of ghoulish nausea.
The memory of her smells like daunting liquor whose touch
happily inebriates me though I cripple before her excesses.

Her lips left a mark on me just frivolous enough
to be called young. Gargoyles and goyim frighten the tongue,
such saccharine hands,

Rubbing my coiled and coiffed face
It was dizzy being so stumbled in love.

VI

The night is tormented in apple scraps
pear pits and dribbled wine streams
all dried out and impossible to clean.

Eliminating everything, I drink myself in rain
to a polluted half-sleep of ribald reveries with the goy.

The moon smokes his motley cigar
dripping with acerbic nectar.

Come colocynthis to my tawdry garden
to be planted by my bloodied hands.

VII

This is the night I bid farewell
to the preponderance of purple
vagabond hopes to determine
how she quarantined me

I lie drunk in another man's arms
petrified of the stains from her angel kiss,

Clinging to my mask
I staple myself to the sky.

Oh fortress of demolition bedridden
with the belfries sounding out haunting calls
about the meaning of my stone cheekbones.

As other cries and whispers emerge from my slim memories of you
the sound of your passionate calls of my name
echo in my head

Onigawara? onigawara?

~ Frank Heather
New York, USA

Undead Blackberry Brandy Tea

Get It

14 oz Sweet Tea

1 ½ oz Blackberry Brandy

1 oz fresh Blackberry Puree

Fresh Blackberries

Mix It

1. Mix tea, brandy and puree.

2. Serve over ice.

3. Top with fresh blackberries.

Read It

Ooh, get ready for another love story. This one stars a beautiful girl and a creature of the night. We ladies sure do love our bad boys! Think ahead and make this a double. One for you and one for your night-born horror...

Nosferatu

Midnight outside of my boutique,
I saw them photographing me
working on each treasured antique
from many a fine century.

They seemed happy, perhaps just met
upon these ancient cobblestones,
this handsome man and sweet coquette
capturing pale flesh on old bones.

Then moonlit truth was soon revealed
upon my waiting room's mirror,
a dark fact no longer concealed,
her beau was a night-born horror.

I think he sensed the change in me
as my heart drummed furiously
he pulled her quickly down the street
to vanish mysteriously.

I searched for them until the dawn,
at last accepting they were gone,
wondering if she was victim
or chose to be his undead spawn.

~ Michael H Hanson
New Jersey, USA

Redcap Zinger

Get It

8 oz Fresh Lemonade

8 oz Sweet Tea

2 oz Fresh Raspberry or
Strawberry Puree

Mix It

1. Mix lemonade and sweet tea.

2. Pour over ice.

3. Top with raspberry or strawberry puree.

Read It

Can't sleep at night? Restless souls make easy prey, but a batch of zinger may keep the redcap at bay. What? Y'all should know by now that I don't write poetry. I leave that to all you Beasties and Ghouls out there. And this next one? It's like an after midnight date with destiny...

Redcap

Redcap creeps along
late night country roads,
searching for that yellow glow,
the broken sleep of restless souls
awake when all the rest
have surrendered to the land of dreams.

Redcap breathes in heavy gasps,
halts and heaves,
his insides dying,
the red cap drying in the wind,
the need to whet his red cap's appetite
for blood a cruel necessity.

And so, at last, he stops to gaze,
outside a lonely farmhouse
kitchen window frame,
the tinkling of a tea cup
signaling an after midnight
date with destiny.

~ Kurt Newton
Connecticut, USA

Whispering Moonlight

Get It

1 Tbsp Dried Chamomile Flowers
1 Tbsp Dried Lavender Flowers
1 Tbsp Raw Honey
2 oz Whiskey

Mix It

1. Steep chamomile and lavender in hot, not boiling, water for 10 minutes.
2. Remove tea bags or strain; add honey and whiskey.
3. Serve warm or chill and serve over ice.

Read It

Being dead and all, I'm accustomed to the dark. It's not as bad as most of y'all think and this tea should help you relax a bit. But, ya know those times when you get a quick shiver as you're making your way through the dark? Almost like a feeling of being watched? Yeah, ya might want to scurry a little faster next time because you probably are...

The Night Whispers

The night whispers, dark and dim;
the moon is perched upon a rim
of hazy clouds and glowing stars,
its beams trailing in thin bars
through the window panes and screens
of sleeping people, passing unseen
and casting shadows on the walls,
in bedrooms and silent halls,
voiceless forms that cavort and play
and vanish in the light of day.

The wind travels, soft and chill,
going when and where it will
and stopping when it wants to stop;
a soft rain falls, drop by drop,
a fine mist spreading in the air,
leaving puddles here and there
that splash beneath some lover's feet
as they're hurrying to meet

their partner in some light's warm glow,
away from all that they don't know
that lives and lingers in the dark,
in silent streets and empty parks.

Claws click on slick cobblestones,
the breath of some beast yet unknown
steaming in the freezing air
like some phantom to beware;
it waits for the night to come,
when its work can all be done,
where moonlight spills in silken reels
on darkness nipping at men's heels,
and even when the work is done
the night whispers on and on.

~ Sarah Cannavo
New Jersey, USA

Lost Princess

Get It

8 oz Hot Water
1 tsp Chamomile Flowers
1 tsp Peppermint Leaves
1 tsp Lemon Balm
1 tsp Crushed Rosemary
1 Tbsp (½ oz) Raspberry Syrup
8 oz Orange Pellegrino® (optional)

Mix It

1. For hot tea: Steep herbs in hot water for 15 minutes. Add raspberry syrup and serve warm.
2. For iced tea: Allow herbs to steep in hot water until water cools to room temperature. Add raspberry syrup; stir in Orange Pellegrino®. Serve over ice.

Read It

Unrequited love is the worst. To love someone who never quite loves you back, torment. Despair at its darkest. Not that I'd know or anything. Oh, damn, I think I got a bit of that peppermint in my eye. Really. That burns. Brew an extra cup of this tea, hot or iced, and reach out. Maybe she'll find the love she longs for...

A Witch Reflects on Loss

I

Aurora was my first.
She was eager to learn…
Magic, mystery, mayhem…
Her trembling beauty,
Wide-eyed innocence,
Lips parted in wonder.
Those infinitely kissable lips.

It wasn't spite that made me prick
Her finger with that spindle…
I wanted her to live forever—
Always seventeen.

II

Rapunzel, in her tower,
Seemed a second chance.
I could raise her as I wanted,
Teach her ways of love,

Be there for her when
She needed comfort.

But the blushing cheek of an errant lad
Drew her away from me
So quickly that she never
Saw my tears.

M

Snow White seemed poised to be the one…
She was witty and charming,
She was eager and loving,
She was everything I needed
With none of the baggage…

Little did I know she came with her
Own cadre of bodyguards.
We were never alone.
The apple was meant for Bashful,
Who shadowed her the most.

I just wanted to get her alone…

IV

And now, I sit beside the sea…
A sad reflection of the witch I was.
All my girls gone from me…
Taken by princes to become other.

I hear the sad song of a mermaid
Seeking enchantment…
Tonight I light a candle,
And hope it draws her here.

One last try to find the arms
I long for.
One last hope that love can see
Beyond the mask.

What is there to lose in the trying?

~ Rie Sheridan Rose
Texas, USA

Iced Brazilian Cha Mate

Get It

2 Tbsp Erva-Mate Tea Leaves
16 oz Hot Water
Sweetened Condensed Milk

Mix It

1. Steep tea leaves in hot water for 5 minutes, covered.
2. Drizzle with sweetened condensed milk and serve.

*Iced Tea Alternative: Steep in 8 oz hot water; drizzle with sweetened condensed milk; add 8 oz cold water and ice.

Read It

Hey, y'all see that short dude over there with the orange hair and backwards feet?Stay away from him, my friends. He'll steal away what little sanity you have left. But if you happen to cross his path, bring him a chá mate and maybe you'll be spared his wrath...

Backward Footprints

Over the forest treeline, see?
Some kind of superimposed Oz
Follow those footprints my friend
and you shall see it...

Confused? It's the beginning silly.

Now your ears must bleed
from the piercing whistling sound
trickling down your stained sideburns

It stands there now, glaring.
blistering skin, bright orange hair
and its feet turned backwards

"Fear me," the creature says

Hysteria, madness clouds your being
death crosses your sight like
a flash of blinding light.

Next time you'll remember, huh?
you mean old hunting man
don't hunt our forest dwellers

Or face the wrath of
Curupira of the Brazilian forest.

~ Donald Armfield
Massachusetts, USA

Scottish Kelpie Secret Tea

Get It

2 Tbsp Black Tea Leaves
1 slice Unpeeled Apple
1 slice Fresh Rhubarb
2-3 oz Oat Milk

Mix It

1. Bring 16 oz water, apple and rhubarb to a boil, cover and simmer for 10 minutes.
2. Remove from heat. Add black tea leaves, cover and steep 10 minutes.
3. Strain into cup. Top with fresh oat milk.

Read It

Y'all better heed the warnings your old granny gives you. Her granny gave them to her and her granny—well, you get the idea. You don't want to end up like Cousin Dudley, do you? He never heeded the warnings. Come to think of it, he was a bit of a whiner anyway...

Secrets of the Loch

There's death waiting for you, child,
You mustn't ever stray
Into the shadows of the loch;
That's where the kelpies play.

Daylight won't protect you, no,
They'll act like your best friend;
Invite you to ride, bareback, laughing,
As you meet your bitter end.

There's death waiting for you, child,
And they've done this before;
The kelpies steal the children,
Leaving their innards on the shore.

Heed my warnings, little one,
It's best you stay away;
The loch can keep its secrets,
And you'll live another day.

~ JR Bournville
East Ayrshire, Scotland

Luring Temptation Tea

Get It

2 Tbsp Orange Pekoe Tea
½ tsp Vanilla Extract
½ tsp Almond Extract
2 oz Orange Blossom Honey
2 oz Milk

Mix It

1. Steep tea in 10 oz hot water for 5 minutes.
2. Add extracts and honey.
3. Pour into mug and top with milk.

Read It

How many times do I have to tell ya not to go into the woods alone? Y'all never listen, especially when a beautiful woman is involved. Listen. Just because a naked siren is luring you and tempting you, doesn't mean you should. All you get is dead...

A Siren's Pursuer

A seductive hymn within the after hours
enchants in call to woo
fluttering over the sleepless rest.

Following the feathers descending from
the canopy of the black forest,
in search of the lovely voice.

The omen of impending death
ticks from within the wood, the deathwatch beetle
portending the pursuer of a closed curtain ahead.

At the bank by the open sea
her wing span closes over her naked body,
and dissolves into her skin.

She smiles at her pursuer,
he's transfixed by her slenderness
but yet, lost by the water's edge.

Before the twilight hours
the siren's pursuer is deprived
voice and sight in destruction alike.

Waves return and love flies
as talons are to catch its prey.
One must not be fooled by temptation.

~ Donald Armfield
Massachusetts, USA

Wild Werewolf Chai

Get It

2 Tbsp Oolong Tea

1 sprig Fresh Tarragon

1 pod Cardamom

½ Cinnamon Stick

3 whole Cloves

1 slice Fresh Ginger

1 oz Honey

⅛ tsp Tamarind Paste

⅛ tsp Almond Extract

⅛ tsp Vanilla Extract

2 oz Sweetened Condensed Milk

2 oz Coconut Milk

Mix It

1. Bring 16 oz water to a boil and remove from heat.

2. Steep tea leaves, tarragon, cardamom, cinnamon, cloves and ginger for 10 minutes, then strain.

3. Add honey, tamarind paste, extracts and condensed milk; stir until dissolved and well combined.

4. Drizzle with coconut milk. Serve hot or over ice.

Read It

Hunger is a powerful need. It can drive the mildest of beasts to uncontrollable behavior. This chai is sure to satisfy any wild craving...

Hunger

Slowly, desire builds up
Insinuating a personal fear
Reality proves only truth
Spasms rock through muscle

Gazing toward the moon
Leisurely, skin slides open
A new form protrudes
Clarity intertwines with distortion

Hunger for your thoughts
Hunger for your words
Hunger for your flesh
Hunger for the madness

Instantly, humanity becomes lost
All parts are false
Sewing life's new plan
You can't run away

Grasping your beating heart
Needing to crush it
And it is inevitable
Even with loving you

Leaves crunch across ground
Dead flowers tear through
Uncontrollable cravings fiercely ensue
Loudly, howling at night

~ Candace Robinson
Texas, USA

Strawberry Rooibos Soul Eater

Get It

2 Tbsp Red Rooibos Tea
6 large Fresh Strawberries
2 slices Fresh Orange
2 oz Clover Honey
1 Cinnamon Stick
Half-and-Half

Mix It

1. Add tea, strawberries, orange slices, honey and cinnamon to 16 oz boiling water; steep covered for 5 minutes.
2. Strain and cool to room temperature.
3. Pour over ice and top with half-and-half. Garnish with strawberry and orange slices, if desired.

Read It

Ooh, I just love a good bedtime story! Now, where did I leave that glass of water? I wonder if tea works just as well...

The Novealla of Vuorwro (#6)

I've never read a poem
about the throats of ghosts,
but my Sámi blood aches
to tell you, no, warn you,
of the thick thirst the dead
have for our hintings of breath,

The way that we seem so dead
yet alive in our sleep, a perfect
balance between this world
and the next, and I imagine
Vuorwro standing, no, floating
above us in our sleep, admiring

Our necks, hearing the theater
of our hearts, sensing the heat
of our skin, and then realizing

That she can bathe in our blood
faster than we can wake.
Vuorwro can only eat souls

Of those who have no water
in their rooms; this is the myth,
no, the story, the story told

As true in my youth, of her mouth,
the way it can open, tongue out,
the voice of her teeth speaking,

The sound of her slaughter, a sickness
of doom, the tingling of her night—

Wandering, as she goes from room
to room, her avant-garde hair

A tangle of angry language, and
a final warning from my mother,

That if you have a cup of water
and feel safe, never look out

Your window at the sky, caught
up in what you might think

Is a reindeer floating across
the starred black, only to have

Her shift form, the window open

Like a mouth and suddenly your

Soul is sucked, like from a straw,

And you are pulled into Hell.

This was our bedtime story,

No, myth, no, warning of the war

Between the corporeal and the non-,
how we should be aware
of being fish-hooked by blood,
turned to blood, cooked in blood,
if we do not keep our blood
true as the iciest north winds.

~ Ron Riekki
California, USA

Chimera Freedom Tea

Get It

1 Tbsp Green Tea
1 Tbsp Dried Chamomile
1 Tbsp Honey
2 oz Passion Fruit Juice
2 oz Blood Orange Juice
Fresh Strawberries

Mix It

1. Combine passion fruit and blood orange juice; pour into ice cube trays and freeze.
2. Steep tea, chamomile and honey in 16 oz hot water, covered, for 20 minutes.
3. Pour warm tea over passion/orange ice cubes, top with fresh strawberry.

Read It

Fantastical creatures can be magnificent, elegant in their form alone. But hey, like the rest of us—living or dead—they can be pretty grumpy upon waking. I guess being frozen in rock for centuries can leave anyone a bit weak and traumatized. This tea aught to help her relax and chill out a bit...

Figment Fantastica

Moonlight touches gently down
to land on terrible remains of
beast in boneyard everstill
yet tremors harbor future woes

No sound shifts silent majesty
as nighttime holds its breath to wait
and wait again then willingly
to sacrifice to Dawn's true might
and safety bought supremacy

The pitiful chimera
turned to stone by
Gorgon's hateful glare
stands gaitless for eternity
with acid rain and heartless wind
upon a ruined tapestry

Its wings once strong
and loathsome now

lay broken useless,
lifeless at the
yellow taloned feet below
like moths caught in blue agony
to crumble in a sizzling heap

Its once proud beak
now stump and perch
for scornful birds to
feed and preen and
roost within its armory
now hollowed raw
a harmless host to augury
which but ignored speaks warning words

But proudful eyes
tend only that
which prized and praised
to seek the ways which boast
of heartless ruler be
of night and light and
all between once tempered by
a terrors reign
forgotten now in Spring's soft ways

Avoiding signs of growing thaw
to crack the stone and
soon reveal vile dread reborn
with wings reformed and sharpened beak
to rend and tear and victims
seek among the innocents who live
in vale and loch and glen and dale
for winter's breath seeks like to like
and frees from frozen stone of aught
a horror brought unknowingly

And so soon now a Queen returns
with demon's claw
and eagle's beak
like sharpened shells of barnacle
and wings of membrane poisoning
those lodged within the hateful space
now space no more for heart replace
and breast regrown
and lion's jaw to rip anew
a maiden's hope who sees her
loved one torn from life

So take no peace
from dreamless sleep

or gentle warmth
or lover's touch
or mother's milk in loving arms
For soon comes that which
nightmare bears upon the wings
of sanity's last gossamer
which holds it firm and now
released to free the beast once
trapped by glare of gaze to snare
by Gorgon's hatred now long dead

Her eyes no longer there to trap
and freeze to leave
an evil bound unknowingly on
same sides were unholiness
and deaths true kiss once
strangers yet of goal the same
to hurt and purge the green remains
and all those habitating there
to season fear with hopeless plight
endeavoring to live despite
anathema's unyielding touch
a bane existence
still to wield

And so a warning all do heed
Chimera's obscene rule begins
anew once mirrored freedom brings
release to she thought long since gone
a shimmering of hatred bound

~ Taye Carrol
Illinois, USA

COCKTAILS & MIXED DRINKS

Y'all know what's better than an amusement park (which isn't really amusing or a park, is it)? A glimpse behind the veil of mortal normality, without the expense of a hospital bill and a near-death experience, of course.

Here you'll encounter spooks, specters, ghouls, demons and just the plain weird. On this strange journey through cocktails and mixed drinks, y'all are going to see things that twist your perception of the world and may cause you to call into question your own sanity.

Or maybe it's just the alcohol talking.

Enjoy, y'all!

The Drinks

The Kraken

Blue Lagoon

Lost At Sea

Black Widow

Cherry Wine
Disguise

Thieving Fairy

Goblin Sedator

Bruja Potion

Spirit Bloom

Frozen Bloody
Vampire

Lambton Worm

Zombie Tamer

Rural Hag

Monster Metaphor

The Poetry

The Seafloor God by Ethan Hedman

A Kelpie's Promise by Trisha Wooldridge

Siren's Song by LS Reinholt

Widow's Weeds by Linda Lee Ruzicka

Skin Walking by MF Senger

Stolen by Jillian Bost

Bedtime by Lynne Sargent

The Witches Give Birth by Joshua Lupardus

The Rattling Tree by Rob E Boley

The Confession by Timothy Tarkelly

An' I'd Swally the Little Bairns by Kimberly Brannon

Plague Ship by Emerian Rich

Death by Breaths by Gerri Leen

Eternal Epitaph by Don Campbell

The Kraken

Get It

1 oz Spiced Rum
1 oz Absinthe
2 oz Tonic Water
1 tsp grated Fresh Ginger
1 slice Lime

Mix It

1. Combine rum, absinthe, tonic water and ginger; shake well.
2. Serve over ice with a slice of lime.
3 *For those who care not of the condition of their liver, substitute tonic water with chilled Crabbies Ginger Beer.

Read It

Now, I know y'all have heard the saying *let sleeping dogs lie*. Well, that goes double for krakens. Those dudes are cranky as hell when pulled from sleep. I was too, but dying was a wonderful cure for that. You can get so much done when you're well rested. It's wild...

The Seafloor God

Beneath the surface of the waves
A creature slumbers well
Within a dark and sunken cave
Too low to feel a swell

Just one thing ails this seafloor god:
An intermittent wake
Should a ship sail above and plod
The creature's wrath will quake

And so the wind can curse a crew
Unlucky to move slow
These ships which churn and muddle through
The kraken's wrath will know

Its trunk-like tentacles shall thrash
Against any such foe
The thickest hulls will break and splash
Into the depths below

No man has lived to tell the tale
Their secrets lost at sea
The wreckage hides under its veil
All far too deep to see

The kraken slips back to its home
And slumbers like the dead
Awaiting the next pile of bones
With which to make its bed

~ Ethan Hedman
Florida, USA

Blue Lagoon

Get It

1 oz Brandy
2 oz Spiced Rum
1 oz Blue Curaçao
½ oz Lime Juice
Fresh Lemon

Mix It

1. Shake brandy, rum, curaçao and lime juice.
2. Pour over ice.
3. Garnish with fresh lemon.

Read It

Follow your dreams, they say. Well, whoever said that clearly never met a kelpie. They're the most deceitful of creatures. Luring you in with dreams—dreams from which you may never awaken. So, sure. Follow your dreams, but seriously, y'all need to stay out of the water. And if you find yourself caught in one of those kelpie dreams, just face it—you're not waking up so enjoy it with a Blue Lagoon...

A Kelpie's Promise

A puddle appeared in the valley.
    And grew
to not quite a pond
but enough of a hazard
where warnings were issued
    of drowning
    should someone follow
    mysterious hoof prints
and take a wrong step on sodden ground.

Muggy twilights brought a salty brine
texture, smell, taste to the air.
Some said it
    made them think
of wild childhood vacations
    on the sea.
Fantasy waves
as they'd never seen the coast
    in all their lives.

Some who said so, though,
        had not lived long enough
to have left childhood.
Still, even children
        have their unfulfilled fantasies.
And lack of age
        does not negate
        the ache
        of what longing lacks.

Others, older others,
        said those humid
        fleeting dusks
of soft light and vivid horizons
        smelled of sex
        and sweaty bodies' promises,
of a different kind of wild
        a different lap of waves.
Still a longing for lack of something.

A something that lived
        only in the memory
        of dreams.

Dreams came; they did.
        On trotting hooves.
The toss of a midnight mane
        full of promise,
        a fantasy of freedom.
That perfect pony prancing to a portal
        to a place where one is
        secretly a prince or princess
        or pirate
        or pauper-turned-hero.
Protagonist of your personal Neverland.
What child won't ride this pony
        who waits patiently
        and without judgement?
No matter how awkwardly you climb upon its back.
        You won't fall.

That stallion waits.
        A different dream.
        A different promise
in his dark hair and moonlit, sparkling, ocean eyes
        of freeing waves
to fix your unfulfilled fantasy.

He doesn't judge.
    And patiently waits for
    your eager "yes."
He welcomes your mount;
    nothing feels awkward.
And you welcome his bucks.
He won't let you fall.

With each disappearance,
    a search party goes out
and carefully treads on sodden ground,
finding only the pond has shrunk—
    to puddle
    to nothing
but blood red mud
that clings to their boots
    and drips like children's tears.

~ Trisha Wooldridge
Massachusetts, USA

Lost At Sea

Get It

4 oz Light Rum
1 oz Fresh Lime Juice
1 oz Maraschino Cherry Juice
1 oz Vodka
1 Tbsp Raw Sugar
1 Tbsp Blue Sugar Sprinkles

Mix It

1. Add sugar and sugar sprinkles to the bottom of a glass.
2. Shake rum, lime, cherry juice and vodka with ice.
3. Pour into glass and serve with a slice of lime and a Maraschino cherry.

Read It

Those pesky sirens. Damned if you do, damned if you don't. I wouldn't want to be caught by one but hey, if you're going to be lost at sea, may as well enjoy the beautiful gifts and charming voice while you can. I don't know about you, but it's times like this I sure am glad to be dead. The downside? There aren't too many sailors around here...

Siren's Song

Come to me and see I offer
Gifts beyond your hopes and dreams
Knowledge of all words and powers
Dance with me on moonlit beams
I will take you in my arms
And charm you with rapturous bite
Joined the minds will be eternal
Souls forever caught in flight

Sailor in your boat so proud
Don't pass me by here on my reef
Losing me will lend you life
But buy you unremitting grief
What is found on Siren's Shore
Once glimpsed can never be forgot
Everything your heart desired
Lost at sea and come to naught

Angler cast your net, these waters
Teem with more than scaled prey
In my bosom you will drown as
Inscience is kissed away
Sinking into wells of wisdom
Pilgrim, home where you belong
Sailors find their final shore
Consumed at last within my song

~ LS Reinholt
Ryomgard, Denmark

Black Widow

Get It

1 ½ oz Vodka
2 oz Half-and-Half
6 oz Dr Pepper® Soda
¼ oz Cherry Syrup

Mix It

1. Shake vodka, half-and-half and cherry syrup with ice.
2. Pour into a tall glass.
3. Slowly add soda and serve.

Read It

So many spiders make their home in the Machleif Cemetery, spinning gorgeous webs, creeping through the night, watching over the Beasties and Ghouls that live here, frightening away the outsiders. But none are so lovely and beautiful as the black widow with her hourglass shape, long legs and deadly venom. What more could you ask for in a girl? Oh, did y'all know a female's venom is fifteen times more toxic than a prairie rattlesnake? These are some sexy ladies you definitely don't want to piss off...

Widow's Weeds

As I walk behind the horse drawn hearse
glass sides shine in the sunlight,
within lies my dear departed husband
after barely a year of marriage has passed

The ebony gossamer veil flutters against my face
blinds me, lifts and lets me see again
as ostrich feathers stir, lightly trailing
their trembling touch against my neck

I am widowed, how this came about, I know not
for he was the most robust of men
my love was young, fit, strong and hearty
but he wasted away, slowly day by day

We were so much in love, he and I
sharing passionate kisses throughout the night
which he swore he could not recover from
and sometimes I wonder, I wonder....

For when donning my black widow's weeds this
    morn,
I glanced down at my smooth pale abdomen
at the birthmark, which is mine, as was
my mother's and her mother's mother

Two blood red triangles, hourglass shaped,
which now glowed in the morning light
as I lightly traced them with my fingertips
leaving a slight shiny trace of webbing behind.

~ Linda Lee Ruzicka
Pennsylvania, USA

Cherry Wine Disguise

Get It

4 oz Cherry Wine

4 oz Cherry Cola

Mix It

1. Fill a glass with ice.
2. Add cherry wine and top with cherry cola.
3. Stir gently and enjoy, but take care. It will sneak up on you.

Read It

There are all kinds of Beasties and Ghouls out there. Some let you know who they are and others—others hide behind a familiar face, wearing a mask that isn't their own at all. And there are those who take "walking a mile in someone else's shoes" to a whole new level. If y'all need a quick disguise, I suggest this cherry wine cola. After a few, you'll feel like a whole new person, barely able to recognize yourself. And ya even get to keep your own skin...

Skin Walking

Strip, grip, rip, drip.

Green like the late summer trees, we were naive,

We believed—ghosts, lycans, witches we were—asleep

On rough-cut uneven ground, hearing sounds, swallowing fear
   down

inside the camping tent. The smell of copper—no, electricity—no,
blood.

Strip, grip, rip, drip.

Sun setting, we'd seen in the cove of trees a man, hunched down
   on haunches—

An animal, but we leave before he launches.

He stared with bare eyes, bare body, bared smile.

(What is he smiling for?)

Strip, grip, rip, drip.

Sunrise, surprise ignites our eyes, we tell lies, at least, that's what
   the grownups think,

"There was a man, a man in our camp last night."

Didn't know they tossed the baby out with the kitchen sink.

Dying fire, out of wood, we would, wouldn't we? go into the
        woods, collect some kindling,
Bring our dad, kin thing. Kinderling, we run off ahead but return
        to that smell,
like copper, like ozone, like blood, we run back, a shell
stands before us, bruised body, bloody, beaten, bare eyes wide.

Strip, grip, rip, drip.
"You okay?" "You okay?" he repeats, he repeats, he repeats.
Back at camp, he stares into the woods, and when no one looks,
He raises his head back and laughs, silently, bare eyes, bared teeth.
(What is he smiling for?)

Strip, grip, rip, drip.
Home, he would rather return to the woods, and maybe one day
        he would,
Because when he leaves, I hear the words "skin walker" in that
        order
And I know my father would never have walked out on me,
but something walked in and walked his skin
back to from where it came to be.

~ MF Senger
Illinois, USA

Thieving Fairy

Get It

2 oz Grappa
1 oz Sloe Gin
1 oz Blood Orange Juice
1 tsp Fine Granulated Sugar

Mix It

1. Combine ingredients in shaker with ice.
2. Strain into a chilled glass.
3. Garnish with a maraschino cherry.

Read It

I know y'all think fairies are cute and fun, but looks can be deceiving and y'all don't know them very well. Never judge a book by its cover—or a fairy by its wings. Thieving is wrong, y'all know that, right? I mean, sure, some things are more valuable than others but nothing is safe when fairies are around. Some like shiny pretty things, like jewelry and stones and other trinkets. The tooth fairy, she'll steal your teeth for the gnomes. They're harmless. And contrary to what you Beasties and Ghouls like to believe, fairies don't steal your socks from the dryer. Y'all might want to keep a better eye on your children though...

Stolen

The child's laughter freezes her heart;
Like snow adrift it blows through the house.
No child, but a creature, haunts her now
In place of the one she held at her breast.

She covers her fingers and wrists in iron,
Hangs a heavy ring around her burning neck,
Praying she will conquer the usurper
Who longs to steal her milk for its own kin.

The fair folk taunt and smash and scream and break,
Scaring the horses and souring the cows,
But still she holds fast to the faith of her love,
And of her blood, even as the fair folk foul.

~ Jillian Bost
Berkshire, UK

Goblin Sedator

Get It

¾ oz Gin
¾ oz Sweet Vermouth
¾ oz Fresh Lime Juice
¾ oz Orange Liqueur
¾ oz White Absinthe
Orange Bitters

Mix It

1. Pour a dash of orange bitters into a chilled glass; swirl to coat the inside.
2. Shake gin, vermouth, lime, orange liquor and absinthe with ice.
3. Strain and pour into coated glass. Garnish with a slice of lime and orange peel.

Read It

Goblins sure can be a tease. Ya know, they're a lot like sour patch kids. First they're sour, then, well, then it's too late to be sweet. On second thought, they aren't really like them at all. They're a bit more like hot tamales or fire balls. The kick sneaks up on you and then it really is too late...

Bedtime

I tuck my goblins into bed.

"The rest is for tomorrow,
it will not be forgotten,"
I sing; I appease.

I fold the covers around them
so they will fear no loss tonight,
so no shadows will enter their sheets.

So they will not run wild and infect the hours
with fever dreams. So they will not
pinch toes and flicker lights and itch.

So they will not moan or tingle or tie my ankles
with the bedsheets. So they will not
send pins and needles into my arms and my spine
and leave me paralyzed with all the words left unsaid.

Instead, they will drift off to the lullaby
and tomorrow I will let them consume me
like waffles. I will let in the daylight.

I will let my skin catch on fire.
We will listen to the crackle and hiss of its song together

~ Lynne Sargent
Ontario, Canada

Bruja Potion

Get It

1 oz Stega
1 oz Tequila
1 tsp Lemon Juice
1 tsp Lime Juice
1 Tbsp Orange Juice
1 tsp Fine Granulated Sugar
8 fresh Mint Leaves
5 fresh Raspberries
Green Maraschino Cherry

Mix It

1. Combine all ingredients with ice and shake.
2. Remove mint leaves and pour over crushed ice.
3. Garnish with a green maraschino cherry

Read It

Legends often serve as warnings not to stray from the good and the rightous because horrible things result from indulging the darkness inside you. Oh, come on, y'all really think I believe that? Embrace the darkness within. I do. But never, never, never trust a witch...

The Witches Give Birth

In the deep, deep darkness of the woods
Three warty women by a cauldron stood,
Their skin was pale, a ghoulish green,
Slime-like sweat made them gleam.
They stirred the pot that bubbled so,
"Tail of newt, now in you go."
They cackled and laughed under the moon,
Their hands all stirring, preparing their brew.
When the fire died out and the bubbles had stopped,
The women dipped their cups and took a shot.
The slime dried up and the warts went away
The witches were women, beautiful for the day.

They sought out the men who had wives of their own
To charm and enchant, they'd make them all moan.
Steal them away into the dark of the night,
Until the potion had stopped, they'd not know their plight.
They wore fancy gowns, black as their souls.
One wore a hat, the others had bows.

One found the preacher and led him astray,
Another a teacher whose kids were at play.
The last witch had no luck, no one was biting,
Till she caught the eye of a drunk, a ring he was hiding.
He took two more shots till he didn't care,
He hobbled on over, watching her stare.

The witches went to work, pleasing their men.
Soon they'd be with babies, made from their sin.
The potion worked quick, and their bellies grew.
But the men lay asleep, they never knew.
The witches gave birth before morning light,
To babies of darkness: Pain, Disease, Plight.

~ Joshua Lupardus
Illinois, USA

Spirit Bloom

Get It

4 oz Coconut Cream
4 oz Coconut Water
2 oz Vodka
1 oz Kahlúa®
1 oz Orange Liqueur

Mix It

1. Mix coconut cream and coconut water, pour into ice cube trays and freeze several hours or overnight.
2. Shake vodka, Kahlúa® and orange liqueur.
3. Pour over coconut ice and serve.

Read It

Ya know what really creeps out the mortals? Trees with no leaves, just spooky limbs reachng out to them like long, bony fingers. The leaves have fled and all that remains is their ghosts. Makes them shiver and run in fear, especially at night. Pretty cool, right? Come on, people. Ghosts aren't nearly as bad as y'all make them out to be. You can take my word on that. Some of us just like to party.
#notallghosts #ghostsjustwannahavefun #misunderstood

The Rattling Tree

After the sun saws its circular blade
Into the ribs of the horizon,
Ghosts hang like rotten fruit
From the tree's squiggly branches.

The spirits wear leaves like stylish hats
In the early days of autumn.

Like a pocket full of holes,
The mindless tree demonstrates
the subtle art of letting go.

The ghosts throw the leaves like confetti
In the early days of winter.

The soil freezes, and the tree's fuzzy roots
Mimic stiff corpses snuggled
And tangled in dirty shadows.

The phantoms inflate the leaves like balloons
In the early days of spring.

Worms and bones swim in simmering mud,
While the tree's thousand toes wiggle
And tingle in the swollen rains.

The apparitions treat the leaves like strangers
In the endless days of summer.

Under the heavy sun, the tree grows
Upward, as it always has, since it was a seed
In a dead boy's pocket, eager to taste sunshine

~ Rob E Boley
Ohio, USA

Frozen Bloody Vampire

Get It

8 oz Cherry Tomatoes, frozen
8 oz Natural Tomato Juice
2 oz Vodka
½ oz Fresh Lime Juice
1 tsp Worcestershire Sauce
¼ tsp Tabasco® Sauce
¼ tsp Creamed Horseradish
½ teaspoon Celery Salt
Celery Stalk
Italian Seasoning

Mix It

1. Add frozen cherry tomatoes, tomato juice, vodka, lime juice, worcestershire, tabasco, horseradish and celery salt to a blender; blend until smooth and thick.
2. Pour into frozen glass.
3. Sprinkle with italian seasoning, garnish with celery stalk and serve.

Read It

The thing about safe places? Don't buy it. Evil lurks everywhere and monsters are a deceptive bunch. I get it, we all need someone to talk to and share our secrets with but do so with caution...

The Confession

Inside a cross-tied, curtain-drawn confessional.

A figure reverent and toiled full
with ears to secrets
and eyes to God,
but with a hunger in anxious glow
that has its own agenda.

The visitor shivered
as he slid into the comfy dark
of the confessional booth.
Lean and dry knees burst
against an unforgiving floor,
inviting tears (burning)
and a fear bound with suction.

Priest listening,
visitor pouring,
a tale was told.

"Madness," he confessed,
for his bent and horrid soul
wrought for worse and left
to mend with broken hands.

"Sin," he confessed,
to sooth his hellhound heart,
to placate his senses,
or at least play a louder song.

"A vision," he confessed,
that torments his every hour.
"In sleep," he confessed.
"Awake," he confessed.

A monster, a visceral slug
that walks as man
and drains those in his midst,
of words, blood, and breath.

"With my own eyes," he confessed,
pleading his tenor call
for help, reprieve, and quiet;
an apology for his madness.

"This madness," the confessor already knew
was a paw of devilish fortune,
raking to the center of the dog's mouth.

"It is me," the priest confessed,
lunging through mesh and wood
and claiming a neck
to his undead grin.

~ Timothy Tarkelly
Kansas, USA

Lambton Worm

Get It

1 ½ oz Tequila
1 ½ oz Vodka
1 ½ oz Crème de Menthe
1 ½ oz Fresh Lime Juice

Mix It

1. Mix or shake all ingredients.
2. Serve over crushed ice.

Read It

Did y'all ever see that movie with those large underground desert worms? They caused awful tremors in the ground and eventually evolved to faceless walking beasts and winged creatures that could shoot fire out of their butt. The Lambton worm doesn't fly or throw fireballs—I mean, I'm sure it would if it could but living in a well has its advantages and disadvantages. The worm's wrath and destruction are just as terrifying and deadly as any desert worm. Oh, and then there's the curse. Don't even get me started on that...

An' I'd Swally the Little Bairns

The worm or the snake or the dragon

plucked from the current by

that random bored-with-sermons-boy

hung out to dry while he crusaded Palestine

(and nothin' good ever comes from skippin' church on Sunday)

if I were the wiggle or the hiss or the poison breath

gulping milk and swinging trees like billy clubs

if I crushed knights and tarnished their armor

chewed whole sheep and wrinkled mountains

if I grew too large for the well and accidentally swallowed a cow

I'm sure I'd know better than to fight in the river

I'm sure I'd know better than to fight in the river

if I grew too large for the well and accidentally swallowed a cow

chewed whole sheep and wrinkled mountains

if I crushed knights and tarnished their armor

gulping milk and swinging trees like billy clubs

if I were the wiggle or the hiss or the poison breath

(and nothin' good ever comes from skippin' church on Sunday)

hung out to dry while he crusaded Palestine
that random bored-with-sermons-boy
plucked from the current by
the worm or the snake or the dragon

I should know better than to fight in the river
or vow you should never die peacefully in your bed
you'll never die peacefully in your bed

~ Kimberly Brannon
Texas, USA

Zombie Tamer

Get It

1 oz Light Rum
1 oz Dark Rum
½ oz 151-Proof Rum
½ oz Orange Liqueur
1 oz Orange Juice
1 oz Pineapple Juice
1 oz Papaya Juice
1 oz Passion Fruit Syrup
½ oz Lemon Juice
½ oz Lime Juice

Mix It

1. Shake rum, liqueur and juices in a cocktail shaker with ice.
2. Strain into a tall glass with ice.
3. Garnish with fresh pineapple and papaya.

Read It

Y'all remember history class? Professors going on and on about how the settlers sailed for months to the New Country and how awful the conditions were on those ships. Dysentary, scurvy, starvation. I guess those teachers didn't know there were far worse ways to die. Well, it turns out that citrus isn't just a cure for scurvy. When mixed with large amounts of rum, it also tames those zombies...

The Plague Ship

With a deep groan
The ship moaned.
There was no way out
Nor reason to hope.

Abigail prayed,
Mary sang
And I was left to beg.

The disease.
Flesh eating virus they called it
But as mother passed into death
It seemed just a phase.
From dead to undead.
Flesh to be fed.

She woke moments later,
As if death didn't faze her
Eyes full of craving
And soul past saving.
Her breath ragged and smelling of meat
Skin paste and hair the color of wheat

She bit me first.
Because I was nearest
And then she bit Mary
Because she was dearest.

Patrick ran away
Danny kept us at bay,
But we'd get them both
In the end anyway.

On and on it went
As the boat powered forward
Not a crewman at the helm

And in the deep dark night
The moon shone so bright
Bathing the deck in light

And we sway with the waves
Staring forward.
Always hungry.
Always searching.

~ Emerian Rich
California, USA

Rural Hag

Get It

2 oz Whiskey
2 tsp Fresh Lemon Juice
2 tsp Habanero Honey
⅛ tsp Loose Leaf Earl Grey Tea

Mix It

1. Shake whiskey, lemon juice, honey and loose leaf tea vigorously for 3 minutes.
2. Strain with a tea strainer or spoon and pour into a tumbler filled with ice.
3. Repeat until you run out of coughs, alcohol, or consciousness.

Read It

Tuberculosis used to be a very popular disease. Not so much anymore, but these things come and go. Blocking out the memories of such things will only get ya so far. Sometimes, ya just gotta face it. And when a Rural Hag isn't enough to cure you, well, there's nothing left but to accept your fate and know you won't be alone...

Death by Breaths

It comes, the rattling cough
The blood-spotted rags
Wracking my body, ripping my ribs
I reach for laudanum, weak fingers
Gripping the stopper, turning with pain
Shooting up from joints grown old
Broken and twisted
I look like the gnarled elm
Come, my pretties
Not so effective when doubled over
Hacking life out with each breath

Children run from the blood
Before I have a chance to spill any of theirs

My house, so charming, full of dolls and
Wagons and miniature chargers
Rearing for imaginary battle
Eat up, eat up, laudanum used
On them, not myself

Infused in sweets, the taste overshadowed
By sugar and rich cream
Lapped up by small tongues
Now I cough into my warmed milk
Blood speckling like rippled nutmeg
Crimson sprinkles of leaking life

No one comes to see me
Save the apothecary's boy

Can't kill him or there'd be no more
Medicine, the beloved tincture
That shortens my life even as
It gives sweet relief from the pain
Sending me into dreams that cause
Sweaty chills as I meet the maker of curses
The lord of the witches
As I am judged: death becomes me
Screaming even more so
I dream my future and it is torment

I drink the laudanum anyway
At least in Hell I will not cough alone

~ Gerri Leen
Virginia, USA

Monster Metaphor

Get It

1 oz Jägermeister®
½ oz Vanilla Schnapps
8 oz Cherry Cola

Mix It

1. Fill a tall glass with ice.
2. Add Jägermeister® and vanilla schnapps; stir well.
3. Fill with cherry cola.

Read It

Ah, young love. It can be life-giving or life-changing. Relationships are a lot of work, ya know. Sometimes they work out and sometimes not so much. Ya never know which way it's gonna go—until one of them kills the other. So romantic.
Just like Romeo and Juliet...

Eternal Epitaph

You are a ghoul
in the graveyard
of my past life

The siren who took my soul
with magic potion lips
and black cat sounds

Am I being an ogre
to remind you of the spell
that once spooked both our spirits

We were like bats
fluttering above the zombies
soaring on a warlock's broomstick

Now I'm no better than a ghost
rattling my chains to bemoan
what sank in the quicksand

I'd rather be an imp
putting you in an iron maiden
to revive our skeletons

Instead I limp along like a mutant
wishing he had his banshee back
to spin illusion again

But come to think of it
you actually were a witch
wearing a black widow

Who sank her fangs into my heart
to bleed to death my dream
we would have an afterlife

There is no chance of a phoenix here
because you are the phantasmal wraith
and I poisoned spider in a dungeon

So I guess I'll bury our chimera
which turned out to be a squonk without
a demon's chance at reincarnation

And carry a torch into my skull
wherein lies the specter of a relationship
like cobwebs in a catacomb

~ Don Campbell
California, USA

SMOOTHIES

For all of you who would rather drink your fruits and vegetables, these smoothies are right up your alley. I once overheard a werewolf proclaim that a healthy human a day kept the doctor at bay. Just something y'all might want to consider.

There's no alcohol in this section but watch out—a few of these guests can be downright broody. Dpn't let your guard down and remember: if at any time these Beasties make you feel uncomfortable or you feel like something's following you, there really isn't anything I can do about that.

Just drink your smoothie and hope the vitamins kick in before nightfall.

Enjoy, y'all!

The Drinks

The Four Horsemen

Faceless Yokai

Blackened Night Sky

Magical Rebirth

Full Mango Moon

The Siren Goddess

Wendigo's Reflection

The Poetry

And They Ride by Shana Scott

Nopperabo by Samantha Lienhard

Black Vampire by Lavel Wideman

The War Witch by SL Edwards

The Power of the Moon by Ashley Dioses

Fisherman's Lure by Ken MacGregor

The Beast I Am by Jyothika Aaryan

The Four Horsemen

Get It

16 oz Whole Milk
2 oz Vanilla Yogurt
3 Dates
½ Fresh Peach
1 Banana, sliced and frozen
2 Tbsp Almond Butter
1 Tbsp Cocoa Powder
Handful Ice

Mix It

1. Add all ingredients to blender and blend on high until smooth.
2. Pour into glass and enjoy.

Read It

Aren't horses just the most beautiful creatures you've ever seen? So majestic and graceful. And the way they carry the heralds of the apocalypse is just awe-inspiring. Even so, I'd watch out for these guys if I were you. There's not much they can do to me except, well, turn everything to dust...

And They Ride

The white stallion races over our land,
its mane the wind-swept screams
and falling ash from mindless monsters
we think we control.

The strike of the red mare's hooves
beat into our ears, soaking us
with the hatred its master breathes.

The third stallion, black as the storming skies,
breaks our bodies down with each step.
From our life the rider grows strong,
and we fall to the ground
with souls thinned to dust.

But fall away and hide
before he arrives.

With eyes of hot coal and fingers of warped iron,
the fourth rider cowers all,
even those from whom we run.
Whatever hope we might hold
witnessing the horses of ash, blood, and night
can only be taken in this unholy grasp.

So fear the haze,
fear the uncertainty you feel.
When the pale horse runs its pace,
know that upon its back
Death rides.

~ Shana Scott
Missouri, USA

Faceless Yokai

Get It

12 oz Almond Milk
1 Banana, sliced
2 oz Strawberries
2 oz Fresh Raspberries
2 Dates
1 Tbsp Cocoa Powder
Cinnamon

Mix It

1. Freeze banana, strawberries and raspberries severl hours or overnight.
2. Add almond milk, fruit, dates and cocoa powder to a blender and blend on high speed until smooth.
3. Sprinkle with cinnamon and enjoy.

Read It

Did y'all forget what I said before about not walking around alone at night? If ya have to walk alone, don't go approaching random strangers. Even if they seem familiar and safe. And if ya do, well, eventually you'll see their true face, or lack thereof...

Nopperabo

You walk down the road on a moonlit night.
You walk alone down the street.
But up ahead is a welcome sight:
another traveler to meet.

You walk up to her and ask her name.
She turns around with a smile.
You wonder if she plays an unknown game,
as she stares at you for a while.

Then she lifts her hand and wipes away her face.
You stare in shock at the sight.
Then you turn around, and as she gives chase,
you race on through the night.

Your fear-fueled flight brings you to a man
And he asks you why you fear.
You say what happened, and he says, "Like this?"
And wipes away his face like a smear.

You run away and meet more and more,
The faceless ones of the night.
Their faceless hordes greet you on a tour
of their world of fear and fright.

At last your steps take you to your home,
so you run inside and lock the door.
Now you're safe at last, you're on your own.
It's you and your wife, nothing more.

You try to explain, as you give her a kiss,
about the faceless ones that day.
And she doesn't laugh; she says "You mean like this?"
And she wipes her face away.

~ Samantha Lienhard
Pennsylvania, USA

Blackened Night Sky

Get It

8 oz Vanilla Soy Milk
4 oz Honey Greek Yogurt
2 oz Crushed Graham Crackers
4 oz Fresh Blueberries
2 oz Fresh Strawberries
1 Banana, sliced and frozen
6 oz Crushed Ice

Mix It

1. Blend soymilk, yogurt and graham crackers on medium speed.
2. Add blueberries, strawberries and banana and blend until pureed.
3. Add crushed ice and blend until smooth.

Read It

Ya know, a lot of my vampire friends live here in the Machleif Cemetery but I think being a vampire would suck. Really, never seeing the sunlight, living forever, beng enslaved by the night. Personally, I prefer being dead forever. It's a lot more exciting and I don't have to worry about things like light and crosses and wooden stakes...

Black Vampire

I soar in the tendrums
Of a blacken sky;
I soar the depths of hell which
Keeps me bound.

My skin is black and
My wings span a mighty
Speed to action;
As of my fate breaks the
Shackles which enslaves me.

I was secreted away
From any view man can keep.

Black like the
Night as the forest deep.

Where the light
Cannot touch me.

Or the Cross keel me,
Severs ties of blood.

Black is what I am.

Not a slave, nor animal,
But a vampire. Black.

~ Lavel Wideman,
Tennessee, USA

Magical Rebirth

Get It

4 oz Vanilla Greek Yogurt
8 oz Pineapple Juice
2 slices Pineapple Rings
2 Bananas, sliced and frozen
Nutmeg

Mix It

1. Blend yogurt, pineapple juice, pineapple rings and banana on high speed until smooth.
2. Sprinkle with ground nutmeg and enjoy!

Read It

War is not healthy for children and other living—dead, immortal—things. Being a witch has its advantages, especially when it comes to healing wounds and reviving yourself. Sometimes though, ya just have to die and be reborn in the magical waters if ya want to live forever. If ya ever find yourself at war—with yourself or another—bring along a Magical Rebirth and find your own hidden chamber...

The War Witch

She sinks into the black waters between worlds,
Letting the currents lap her in tendril-curls
As the cool darkness licks her wound
With all the peace of the quiet tomb.

She won't die today, too much to be done.
Demons to slay and wars to be won,
Things to kill in the pitiless sky
Dangerous gods who need to die.

The healing waters fill her flesh,
Entering her gaping, bleeding chest
Tendons crawl together as insect arms
Bring jagged pain and screaming alarms.

The waters take their price, as all things will
And enter her lungs for the final kill.
The cost of her life is only one small death.
So she takes one last, convulsing breath.

She is rebirthed to dim candle-fire,
Alive with furious, burning ire.
The waters have brought her to her hidden chamber
Where she is unbounded and free from danger.

She brings herself to a dark, open pool
To ponder the fate of the little fool
Who has escaped and left her scarred.
Her reflection smiles, now unmarred.

Oh, he was cunning and he was clever
But she is wise, and will live forever.
So she sets to her work, careful and slow
Planting seeds that the decades will sow.

~ SL Edwards
California, USA

Full Mango Moon

Get It

4 oz Passion Fruit Syrup
1 Mango, peeled and sliced
2 oz Plain Greek Yogurt
4 oz Crushed Ice

Mix It

1. Blend all ingredients in a blender on high speed until smooth.
2. Pour into chilled glass and serve.

Read It

Ooh, another full moon. My favorite Beasties always come out to play. Do y'all know how to become a werewolf? You could try being bit by one, or scratched or clawed. That might not work so well but it would definitely hurt. You could try wearing an enchanted wolf-belt, covering yourself in a magic salve, drinking rainwater from a werewolf's footprint or selling your soul to the devil (please, don't do that). Seriously, if y'all want to become a werewolf, all ya gotta do is find a witch willing to give you the curse and then wait for the full moon...

The Power of the Moon

My witch, my lover, spoke a verse
No priest or mage could heal.
I was unfaithful, so her curse
Bestowed a beast to kneel.

The poison of the moonlight flows
Like ice through my thick veins.
The searing pain yet grows and grows,
And every muscle strains.

The stars and planets slowly peek
From out their astral home.
They spot and find what they all seek,
The place the Were will roam.

But when the moon, that orb up high,
Appeared through clouds Yule night,
The wolf inside me knew, and I
Was soon to change outright.

My limbs began to crack and twist,
My teeth grew past my lips,
My bones transformed from foot to wrist,
And then transformed my hips.

The pain coursed like a razor blade,
And all the night heard screams.
I writhed in agony and prayed,
Yet none heard but my dreams.

My tears then bled a grayish blue,
The color of my eyes.
My skin was now a brownish hue,
And hair grew up my thighs.

The agony abruptly stopped—
The aches all went away.
My jaw, at last, aligned and popped—
I was no longer prey.

One instant all the night was still.
I fell into a trance
As I embraced the wolf's fierce will,
I followed Luna's dance.

My senses heightened in the night,
My body moved with stealth;
Reflexes quickened at each sight;
The change improved my health.

My very scream became unknown,
Despite my fierce resistance.
A sound began my path of bone—
Such mirth was in the distance.

I tried resisting, tried to fight;
The curse was stronger, though.
I lost myself in the cold night,
And hunted through the snow.

The hunger and the rage inside—
Like poison, tainted blood.
Something I just could never hide
Washed through me like a flood.

I flew to sounds of laughing souls
Without disturbing stones,
Or leaves atop the darkened knolls,
Or grasses or the bones.

The laughter from a house nearby
Made easy game for me.
And knowing they would all soon die
Aroused me with each plea.

She smiles down, that moon above;
Again the laughter sounds.
Yet not the moon, my witch, my love;
Her icy laugh surrounds.

For such fresh bodies seldom cry
Would this not end so soon?
This curse was made much stronger by
The power of the moon

~ Ashley Dioses
California, USA

The Siren Goddess

Get It

12 oz Almond Milk
1 Banana, sliced and frozen
2 oz Fresh Blueberries
4 Figs
Handful Fresh Spinach
1 Tbsp Almond Butter

Mix It

1. Blend all ingredients in a blender on high speed until smooth.
2. Pour into chilled glass and serve.

Read It

Song can be a beautiful thing unless it leads you astray. Y'all should have listened before when I warned ya about the siren. What is it with you mortals and water? All I can say is drink up before you follow the song...

Fisherman's Lure

You follow my song.

Waves lap at the sides,
Icy tongues hungry for your kiss.
Gulls scream, fighting for scraps.
Shore can't be far.

Row to the gulls,
You think, but you don't.
You follow my song.
Your hands know the way.

You smile, and saliva
Pools in your mouth.
Glass-eyed, you yank
Harder on the oars.

Land-bound, your wife worries.
You forget her.

You see me, finally,
And your grin is Hunger,
Your lust palpable.

You follow my song.

The wood of your prow
Bumps against rock
Where I sit, tail coiled,
Breasts bared, hair flowing.
Your ideal beauty.
You rush to my side,
And I embrace you.

Too late, you smell decay.
Too late, you see the bones
Of those who came before.

You panic, try to flee.
I hold you, and I sing.
You collapse and weep,
You call me "Mommy."

Almost, I let you go.
Almost, I do not feed.

But, I hunger,
And you are here.
You followed my song.

~ Ken MacGregor
Michigan USA

Wendigo's Reflection

Get It

4 oz Plain Soymilk
4 oz Grape Juice
4 oz Pineapple Juice
4 oz Frozen Cranberries
4 oz Dessert Tofu
½ oz Honey
Handful of ice cubes

Mix It

1. Blend all ingredients in a blender on high speed until smooth.
2. Pour into chilled glass and serve.

Read It

You never really know who someone is on the inside until they show you. Don't be surprised if they aren't who you thought they were. Chances are, they weren't who they thought they were either until they break free and see their true reflection...

The Beast I Am

Deafening silence, crimsoned snow, pungent scents
In the wake of screams that swallowed the mountain whole
Hopes, dreams, possibilities
All in the breaths I stole
Reduced to snow angels of flesh and blood
For they meant less to me than my hunger
Hunger that no longer knows satisfaction

Metallic taste on tongue
Not as sweet as it once was
Warmth of flesh waning too quick
For what was it only a blink in the face of my immortality?
For I had renounced my humanity long ago
Almost all
For the shattered screams that ring in my ears
They do not only come from my prey
Rather, from within

A childlike part of me cowers within the depths of my corrupted soul
Trembling fingers gripping innocence I long to kill
Her lips quiver, mortified by how deeply I have slipped
Consumed by inhuman appetites
She desperately attempts to cut me with the guilt I should feel
To remove the poison from the parts that once made me whole
A useless escapade, a mental battle I have no desire in losing
Quiver in voice, she asks how I could trade in so easily
The dreams I once held dear

The mundaneness of mortality, you mean?
My commitment to play the part of a broken beauty?
The porcelain doll cracked in the arms of lovers?
Mortal soul with too much trust in her heart?
Soul sick of trying to see the good in others?

Terror bleeds from every crevice of her small voice
She asks how I could trade the love in my heart for this
A question she asks in the absence of my humanity
I do not care for the way I reek of blood
For the way crimson coats my frayed lips
Of how my hair is no more
For the sallow skin tight against my skeletal form
For pales eyes untouched by sleep
For this beastly curse is now my freedom

She argues, "you are only a bruised soul
That cannot fill the hole with flesh of another
For only your cannibalistic heart will only crave more
Please see the monster you are becoming
For this compared to who you could be
This is not a fair trade!"

Serrated teeth caked with blood, I smile
Her ignorance amuses
My appearance only reflects what always has been within
The beast that grew, inside, waiting, feeding
Strengthened by the pain, betrayal, agony life throws
Merely this is me with removed chains
And the malignant hatred in my blackened heart
It only grows

~ Jyothika Aaryan
New South Wales, Australia

MILKSHAKES

All you hot-blooded creatures need to cool down a bit. Even coldblooded (or in some cases noblooded) creatures love a creamy, rich milkshake on a hot —oh, who am I kidding? I love a good milkshake any day!

But listen, y'all. These aren't your typical frothy treats. These come from hot tempered and short fused creatures and, if you're not careful, y'all might just find something reaching up from the bottom and pulling you in

Alcohol or not, these Beasties are ready to chill!

Enjoy, y'all!

The Drinks

The Drowned Devil

Flaming Night Mare

Wandering Gargoyle

Blackberry Faerie

The Frozen Imp

Grinning Werewolf

Mermaid Matcha & Cream

Woven Silk Spider Egg

Turk Vampir Kahvesi

Cernunnos' Wild Hunt

Guardian of the Forest

Seductive Succubus

Green Monarch Leshy

Carribean Demon Passion

The Poetry

The Scab That Oozes by Nick Manzolillo

Nightmare Upon Dissolution by Jason Ellis

Night On The Town by Andrew Dunlop

The Faerie Rules by MJ Mars

A Prank Too Far by Anne E Johnson

Whitechapel by Samantha Potts

An Vorvoren a Senar by Darren Lester

Frankenspider by Minerva Cerridwen

The Vampire Ogrencisi by Shalom Aranas

Antlered Avenger by Kimmy Alan

Feetures by Shawn Chang

Moon in Purple by Morphine Epiphany

He, The Forest by Jay Outhier

We Are Legion by Allison Shepherd

The Drowned Devil

Get It

9 oz Cream Soda or Root Beer

3 oz Irish Cream Liqueur

16 oz Cookie Dough or
Cinnamon Swirl Ice Cream

Mix It

1. Carefully pour soda into blender.
2. Add irish cream and ice cream.
3. Blend until smooth.

Read It

Nothing ruins a wedding quite like a sad man that just won't stay dead. Following the living around, making a nuisance of himself, dripping on the carpet. Talk about a wedding crasher. Dude, just stay away from the cake and go back to the bottom of the sea...

The Scab That Oozes

There was a man who drowned.

A year later, I saw him again
at my wedding, standing by the cake
flesh washed pale in a suit of seaweed
clutching a ship in a bottle.

He was told to leave and promptly collapsed
into a hastily mopped spillage
of sails, shards and high tide bile.

A big day and an uproarious night
followed by a morning with my head in the toilet.
A damp footprint trail back to bed
the drowned man lingers behind her
whispering a tongue of clicking, starving, jittery crabs
first mistaken for soft waves kissing upon sand

High tide overrides febreeze

The drowned man aches, drying out
he watches our pyrrhic sleep with
clammy sweat rimmed frog eyes
slouching among the ancient wine
stains of the armchair.

I never did learn to swim.

A puddle above drips
missing my outstretched tongue
dribbling along her cheek
I rollover
and lap it away
and I need

I will flick that photo by her bed
and place it down
down by its own weight

I will slither in behind her,
outline her smooth, parting arms
and her powerful kick

I will plug the holes in her nostrils
and kiss the back of her lungs

The drowned man runs a tidal hand
through his hair of eelgrass
belching a point Nemo croak, his gills
appearing like slits along his windpipe

He can adapt,
at the bottom of any sea
But first,
he must search for company

~ Nick Manzolillo
Rhode Island, USA

Flaming Night Mare

Get It

1 ½ oz Fireball® Whiskey
16 oz Chocolate Ice Cream
4 oz Marshmallow Creme

Mix It

1. Add whiskey, chocolate ice cream and 2 oz marshmallow to a blender; blend until smooth.
2. Pour into glasses and top with remaining marshmallow cream.

Read It

Your darkest thoughts can become your worst nightmares. Sometimes those nightmares creep into your waking hours. Sometimes, the darkness consumes all and, well, just take an extra shot of Fireball® while you're making this one...

Nightmare Upon Dissolution

Into my darkest thoughts

Into the darkest night

Nightmare, my guide and my enemy

Nightmare, mane and snort and hoof of flame

Flames, your equine corona

Flames, lapping and leaping with each step

Step, gallop, canter, gait

Step high, step long

Long is our ride through this valley

Long is our ride tonight

Tonight, I grab your mane

Tonight, I sling myself up to our quest

Quest, we shall through many a thicket

Quest, awakening such horrors

Horrors, born of mind and place

Horrors, lapping at my flaming wake

Wake I shall many hours hence

Wake I shall when I am spent

Spent my youth dreaming

Spent my adulthood brooding

Brooding such things as I cannot name

Brooding, toiling, marriage, at sunset

Sunset, I beset my ride

Sunset, for once I will command these dreams

Dreams, long I have had

Dreams, long I have dread,

Dread, we spread dread far and near

Dread, like a disease upon all we pass

Pass the wet nurse's home, the children at play

Pass the old crone's hut and the graveyard still

Still, oh still, we ride despite my terror,

Still, oh still, such stillness outside

Outside of the waking real

Outside of woken thought

Thought only of holding fast

Thought only of this lonely, awful ride

Ride, my nightmare, ride hard through this wood

Ride my thoughts and flay me from my life

Life, so narrow and tiring

Life slipping away from my thoughts as we gallop

Gallop hard, harder still, from my home

Gallop with flaming hoofs thundering

Thundering throughout this valley

Thundering throughout this unstill mind

Mind, awoken, awakening, lost in sleep

Mind, fracturing, disturbed, dissolution

Dissolution, disapparate, dissolve, and disperse

Dissolution, my steed fades once more into darkness

Disperse…

Darkness…

~ Jason Ellis
Kentucky, USA

Wandering Gargoyle

Get It

16 oz All-Natural Vanilla
   Ice Cream
8 oz Guinness®
Dark Chocolate Syrup
White Chocolate Shavings

Mix It

1. Blend Guinness® and ice cream until smooth.
2. Drizzle chocolate syrup down the inside of a tall glass.
3. Pour in shake and top with white chocolate shavings.

Read It

Y'all ever see a drunk gargoyle? No? Really? Let's just say they're not the best tour guides. They really don't hold their liqueur well but they sure do love Guinness®. Perfect for a night upon the town...

Night On The Town

If you travel to the chapel,
On the other side of town,
In the eaves, espy the gargoyles,
Water spouting, never drowned.

See the tall and proud Francisco,
Fierce of face, and wings of stone,
See the horned and snarling Carlos,
See Alberto, all alone.

Named they were by priests and townsfolk,
Sculpted as the beasts of old,
There to drain the eaves and gutters,
As, at least, the story's told.

As the twilight turns to evening,
Darkness falls, and wind blows cold,
Lamplights on their pillars gutter,
Now our story shall unfold.

Sated on credulous tourists,
Stony beasts, their hungers fed,
Moving strangely well for statues,
Stony nature, all but fled.

Still, for all the rainfall guzzling,
Heaven's water, 'nough to burst,
Never sates a statue, truly,
Even gargoyles tend to thirst.

But if gallons from the heavens
Insufficient to the task,
What can slake such pangs in gargoyles?
Gentle reader, surely ask.

Night time now in the old city,
Out around a public house,
Stagger home the weary warriors,
In their stupor, stagger, grouse.

Preyed upon by winged monsters,
Tipsy there, and drunken here,
Not as if the thirsty gargoyles
Could just enter, order beer.

One by one, on drunken walkers,
Gargoyles thirst by liquor quenched,
Sated more on rambling drunkards
Than by rain for years now drenched.

But consider, gentle reader,
As our gargoyles, homeward bound,
Start to sway and wobble gently,
Sober senses, not as sound.

Stop to think; how often really,
Will a gargoyle liquor drink?
Fallen rain no favoured tipple,
Tolerance falls out of sync.

Hard to call a gargoyle 'lightweight',
Made of weighty stuff, they are,
But to see them, stumble-soaring,
Straight to work, that image-mar.

Bobbing, weaving, flying statues,
Hardly graceful, by this time,
Smashed and smashing, clipping buildings,
Terrible, but not sublime.

Come the dawn, and puzzling findings,
When the damage is surveyed,
Explanations are found wanting,
Townsfolk gather, all dismayed.

Leave aside the missing persons,
And the shattered masonry,
Wonder, of these famous gargoyles,
Who moved them so randomly?

First Francisco, proud and mighty,
Dignity is from him stripped,
Found within a pigsty wallow,
Careful stonework cracked and chipped.

Next comes Carlos, fierce and wrathful,
Fountain's statue, he's replaced,
Water spouting up, not outward,
Gargoyle's function, he's disgraced.

Home alone is poor Alberto,
Almost to his post restored,
Somehow he's now facing backward,
From his rear the gutters, poured.

Since the days of Saint Romanus,
Never seen such damage done,
By a bunch of errant gargoyles,
Feasting on townsfolk for fun.

Explanations sought, unanswered,
Infamy, replace renown;
Ne'er again, let gargoyles wander,
For a night upon the town.

~ Andrew Dunlop
Ontario, Canada

Blackberry Faerie

Get It

16 oz Vanilla Ice Cream
8 oz Frozen Blackberries
3 oz Blackberry Brandy

Mix It

1. Blend all ingredients until smooth.
2. Top with fresh blackberries.

Read It

Mmm, I just love fresh blackberries, don't you? So plump and juicy and sweet. You can make them into just about anything—jam, cobbler, muffins, brandy. And a fresh bowl of blackberries makes a gorgeous centerpiece, especially next to a bouquet of fragrant flowers. You can grow them in your own garden or find them growing wild in a field but don't go treading on faerie ground. They have no mercy for trespassers and thieves...

The Faerie Rules

If you come picking blackberries,
    if you come clipping flowers
Know you're in our garden,
    know these woods are ours.
Come with your coat turned inside out,
    come with one sock odd.
Bring silver or a crucifix,
    keep praying to your god.

'Cause when you're in our territory
    the day draws on and on.
Our songs will hold you captive.
    The path you'd walked has gone.
There is no turning back, my friend,
    the forest has you now.
There's no freedom from our garden,
    escape we won't allow.

Follow us to our home, my dear,
    follow us underground.
Listen to our music
    and welcome in the sound.

Stand over in the corner,
    forget the world that's gone.
You're no longer Dad or brother.
    You're no longer someone's son.

You should have left the blackberries,
    you should have dropped the flowers.
You shouldn't have come to our garden
    in the early morning hours.
You should have turned your coat around,
    you should have changed your socks.
God won't help you now, my dear,
    'cause he can't pick our locks.

You came into our territory,
    you came into our home.
The faeries have you now, my friend,
    you'll never be alone.
Stand over in the corner
    and sing our song aloud.
'Cause we're the faeries of the wood.
    And we're your family now.

~ MJ Mars
Lancashire, UK

The Frozen Imp

Get It

2 oz Orange Juice
2 oz Lime Juice
4 oz Pineapple Juice
8 oz Lemon Sorbet
8 oz Vanilla Ice Cream
1 tsp Fresh Ginger, grated
½ oz Honey

Mix It

1. Mix orange, lime and pinapple juices; freeze in ice cube trays.
2. Blend juice cubes, sorbet, ice cream, ginger and honey on high speed until smooth.
3. Pour into glasses and garnish with fresh lime and pineapple slices.

Read It

I love a good prank, don't you? I mean, as long as no one really gets hurt. But ya gotta be careful not to prank the wrong people or take it too far. Payback can be a wee bit painful. Play nice y'all. Don't be an imp...

A Prank Too Far

A wisp of almost freezing wind
Rattled the crisp branches of birch.
Rabbits hunted for leaves
While foxes hunted the rabbits.
The imp hid in a tree hollow, waiting.

The spikes on his wings stabbed beetles
Trying to escape his cloying stench.
The imp flicked their corpses
To the ground and laughed.
"What soft shells you have," he sneered.

Rumor said the Snow Queen was coming.
Of all the tricks the imp had played,
To trick her Majesty
Would be the most glorious.
He wondered though, what prank would prove worthy?

"Tell me what the Snow Queen loves, Owl."
The owl hooted and rotated his head.

"She loves her daughter,
Blue-skinned Princess Crystal,
More than anything. Even more than snow."

Now the imp, with heart twisted and cruel,
Planned a dreadful prank for winter's queen.
"I'll need blood, red as lust,
To set the scene properly."
His taloned hand snatched Weasel's neck and squeezed.

He watched the weasel's blood ooze out
Over a rocky mass of jagged gray quartz.
A wood sprite who feared him
Tinged the rock slightly blue.
The imp bared his sharp teeth in a grin.

"Her Majesty, the Snow Queen," cried Hawk.
"Make way, forest denizens, and bow."
The imp's scrawny legs danced
In anticipation of his prank.
"Oh, queen!" he wailed. "Come quick, my poor queen."

She swept her skirts of winter wheat
To the place where the imp bawled dramatically.
"What is it, lowly Trickster?
Whose blood stains this stone?"
"It is your Crystal's," the imp sobbed. "She is dead."

In the queen's eyes, tears formed and froze.

Her screams crushed the air like a glacier.

Woodland creatures and magic beasts

Cowered behind bushes and boulders.

Even the imp was frightened by the heavens' shaking.

"Gently, queen!" he implored, "'tis but a jest.

This is only weasel blood, not your girl's."

He offered a weak grin,

Which quickly disappeared

When he saw the fury on the Snow Queen's brow.

The queen reached out both ice-pale arms.

A rope of frosty wind bound the imp to a tree.

It burned him until he cried,

"I meant no harm!" She shrugged.

"'Tis but a jest," she said, and walked away.

The imp hangs there still, rotting with regret.

~ Anne E Johnson
New York, USA

Grinning Werewolf

Get It

2 oz Vodka
2 oz White Chocolate Liqueur
2 oz Creme de Menthe
16 oz Vanilla Ice Cream
Grenadine

Mix It

1. Combine vodka, white chocolate, creme de menth and ice cream in a blender; blend until smooth.
2. Pour into a chilled glass; drizzle with grenadine.

Read It

Ya know, I've said it before and I'll say it again. Things aren't always what they seem. And sometimes, ya get exactly what ya deserve. I bet he didn't even see it coming. They rarely do...

Whitechapel

He watched as she laughed like a child,
with friends in company.
He sulked along the darkness rims,
waiting for possibilities.

He thought of how her breath would fade
by his hands around her throat.
He smiled a devilish grin to himself,
as he hugged tightly to his coat.

She looked like a fragile flower,
his favorite kind of delight;
Just waiting to be plucked,
this wonderful moonlit night.

He looked across to the bridge,
where his predecessor met his end.
He wished he could have known the man,
Jack, the faceless legend.

He preferred the face of innocence,
unlike his paragon.
The thrill of stealing virtues,
not just claiming lives alone.

He watched as her friends departed,
one by one they veered;
Until she was all alone,
unto himself he sneered.

She took a turn into an alley,
a perfect time to intercede.
He slowly crept behind her,
his heart began to speed.

Suddenly she turned and looked his way,
he froze there in his place.
She took a step toward him,
he saw the smile upon her face.

His heart steadily quickened,
he felt a change so dear.
The way she slowly moved toward him,
had him trembling with fear.

"Oh, I've been waiting since I saw you,
watching me with great delight.
To taste the blood inside you,
 as I rip apart your life."

She looked up at the moon,
as full as it could be,
softly howling a sweet note,
before devouring her delicacy.

~ Samantha Potts
Mississippi, USA

Mermaid Matcha & Cream

Get It

16 oz Vanilla Ice Cream
2 oz Irish Cream Liqueur
1 Tbsp Matcha Powder
Maraschino Cherry

Mix It

1. Blend ice cream, irish cream and matcha powder on high speed until smooth.
2. Top with maraschino cherry.

Read It

Mermaids have beautiful voices that can make angels weep. But, so can their appetites. Trust me on this one. Make yourself a Mermaid Matcha & Cream, crank up the headphones and stay away from the water...

An Vorvoren a Senar

She appeared one morning in the church,
As beautiful and elegant a woman as I had ever seen.
Hair as golden as the sun
Silk dress, the depth of the ocean's green.

All alone she stood in the choir's stall.
No need of supporting voices.
She opened her mouth and beauty came out,
And the entirety of Heaven rejoices.

She entranced me with her music
and ensnared me with her song.
Her beauty was unparalleled
The pull towards her strong.

She smiled when her tune was done,
She demurely bowed her head.
She looked at me with deep, blue eyes
And smiled with lips bright red.

The next day, I returned to the church
And saw her in the pew.
She sang, like a veery or a mockingbird
And I fell for her anew.

"Forgive me," said I, as she stepped down
And ran fingers through her hair of gold.
"But your voice…it's an…enchantment," said I
Before recoiling for being so bold.

She giggled, she blushed, she patted my arm.
"What a charming lad," she said.
I stuttered. I stumbled. Tripped over my words.
My stomach felt like lead.

I tingled with her hand on mine
Her perfume filling my head.
What was I doing? I wanted to run
Back to my lonely bed.

She smiled, she dazzled me,
Taking my hand and leading me astray.
We ran and kissed and slept and talked
As day became night became day.

"I must show you," she said
On autumn's eve, as the leaves began to fall.
"The most wonderful sight you ever did see.
You'll never wish to leave its thrall."

She led me to the mermaid chair,
the oak so beautiful and strong.
"Sit! Watch!" she instructed me
Before launching into her song.

The stars in Heaven began to shine,
The planets chose to unhide.
The scent of lilies filled the air
As I vowed to make her my bride.

"Come," she sang. "And take my hand.
That water's cool today."
I did not see that her legs did change
As the sky became cloudy and grey.

To me, she was just beautiful,
A goddess in human guise.
Her scales grew up from beneath her skin
And a tempest raged in her eyes.

She led me down beneath the waves
My peril went unseen.
I could feel my lungs begin to burn
As her hair changed from blonde to green.

My lids became heavy, my poor eyes closed
Once more, for the last time.
My body was heavy, it sank to the bed.
And a bell began to chime.

Her sisters emerged from their grottos and caves,
The beauty of woman, the swiftness of fish.
They snipped and snapped at my flesh and bone.
"A young man. The most delicate dish."

"You did well," they praised as they tore my flesh.
"He's tender." "Come, try some thigh."
"They're the most delicious in the village," she said.
"The men of the family Bly."

~ Darren Lester
Gloucestershire, UK

Woven Silk Spider Egg

Get It

4 oz Whole Milk
8 oz Vanilla Ice Cream
1 ½ oz White Chocolate Sauce
½ teaspoon Almond Extract
3 oz Marshmallow Cream
Chocolate and Caramel Syrup

Mix It

1. Blend milk, ice cream, chocolate sauce and almond extract on high speed.
2. Add half the marshmallow cream to the bottom of a glass, drizzle with chocolate syrup, top with half the milkshake.
3. Add remaining marshmallow cream, drizzle with caramel syrup, add remaining milkshake, top with chocolate and caramel syrup and enjoy!

Read It

The itsy-bitsy spider crawled in the vaccuum sack... Listen, y'all need to stop killing spiders. They're beautiful creatures that spin webs and eat other pests. Why would you make yourself a target? Don't be a pest...

Frankenspider

I am legend among spiders
The nightmare in the shed
The slayer with her hurricane
That whirls around the dead.

As I admire my cleaning work
A squirm catches my eye
There's something crawling out the tube
But why didn't it die?

Legs torn apart, the bodies crushed
To dust-and-spider blend
The vacuum takes no prisoners
They've all come to their end.

And yet this thing is twitching back
As soon as I come close
And when I make to hit the switch
The vacuum lifts its hose!

The vessel creaks, the plastic snaps
The sides are soon torn down
Out comes a creature with eight legs
Uneven and gray-brown.

They're splintery, as if composed
Of many smaller shreds
With patchy fuzz all over them
Made up of carpet threads.

As I look on, the monster grows
No longer tight compressed
The cobweb body soon so tall
It comes up to my chest.

It scuttles to me, spits and clicks
Eraser-dust white jaws
And as they close around my thigh
I know I am the cause:

Not emptying the vacuum's bin
The creature grew in there
That now, in vengeance, tears my legs
And whirls them through the air.

~ Minerva Cerridwen
Vlaams-Brabant, Belgium

Turk Vampir Kahvesi

Get It

6 oz Cold Water
2 Tbsp Medium-Roast Turkish-
    Ground Coffee*
12 oz Vanila Ice Cream

* Coffee beans must be ground to
a fine powder prior to brewing.
Use a Turkish grinder or grind
beans at your local grocery store
using the Turkish coffee setting.

Mix It

1. Sprinkle fresh coffee grounds over cold water in a small pot; do not stir.
2. Gently heat water and coffee on medium-high; do not boil or stir.
3. When coffee grounds begin to sink, turn heat to low; stir vigorously until brew starts to foam. Froth as much as possible without boiling.
4. Add ice cream to two tall glasses. Pour Turkish coffee over ice cream, with equal amounts of foam in each and avoiding grounds at the bottom of the pot.

Read It

It's a tale as old as time. Date and ditch. Or, in this case, bite and run. Left alone, lingering, thirsting, wanting more...

The Vampire Ogrencisi

Your Turkish eyes pierced
the locus of my hair
behind my head,
embedded two points
on my neck and forgot
about me,
left to linger the world
with a thirst
to slake for no one
but you.

~ Shalom Aranas
Manila, Philippines

Cernunnos' Wild Hunt

Get It

1 oz Pure Maple Syrup
1 oz Dark Brown Sugar
16 oz Vanilla Ice Cream

Mix It

1. Blend syrup, sugar and ice cream on high speed until well blended.
2. Drizzle additional maple syrup around sides of glass and pour milkshake.
3. Sprinkle top with additional brown sugar.

Read It

Mother Earth sure has got some fierce protectors. None moreso than that half deer, half man they call Herne. What a hottie, that one. Wait? Did I say that out loud? Oh well, mix this up and join Cernunnos' Wild Hunt. Just watch out for those antlers...

Antlered Avenger

An antlered man upon a fire-breathing black horse
To those of evil he shows little if any remorse

Called Wodan by some, and named Herne by others
He calls the fauna and the fawns his sisters and his brothers

Following a pack of Gabriel's snow white Hellhounds
On the gusts of stormy night winds the Heavens he bounds

Any of you who Mother Earth should you offend
He'll snatch up your soul and to Hell he'll condemn

So polluters and poachers you'd better beware
For an antlered avenger rides the night air

~ Kimmy Alan
Minnesota, USA

Guardian of the Forest

Get It

6 oz Avocado

6 oz Mango

2 ½ oz Sweetened Condensed Milk

8 oz Crushed Ice

Mix It

1. Puree avocado, mango and sweetened condensed milk.
2. Add ice and blend on high until smooth and creamy.
3. Drizzle with additional sweetened condensed milk.

Read It

Curupiras, dude. As if the blistering skin and flaming hair wasn't enough, they can hold a serious grudge. But seriously, y'all bring this about yourselves. Stop destroying the forests and killing endangered species. I mean, unless you prefer insanity and death...

Feetures

My voice is like a banshee's, only worse
And deadlier than king cobras in a pit;
To hear me scream will fry your mind and curse
Your sanity so you have no more wit

To call as yours; my feet are more awry
Than the illusions which I cast with glee.
To pique my ire spells suicide by and by,
Your corpse I seek if you dare trigger me;

Atop my trusty beastly ally, friend—
I storm around my forest far and wide.
If you are cruel to creatures I will end
Your foolish life, and nowhere can you hide.

To sink in greed, forget to say your grace
Will send you sprawling into death's embrace.

~ Shawn Chang
British Columbia, Canada

Seductive Succubus

Get It

8 oz Fresh Blackberries
2 Bananas
16 oz Chocolate Ice Cream

Mix It

1. Puree blackberries and bananas.
2. Add ice cream and blend until smooth.
3. Top with one or two fresh blackberries.

Read It

The moon isn't just for werewolves, ya know? The moon brings out all the beautiful, seductive creatures. Mix up a Seductive Succubus and enjoy the fantastic banquet in the moonlight...

Moon in Purple

Between a terrible Moon in purple
and the quiet of roofs in the night chewed
by bad breath of the shadows.

A hysteric squeak coming from the abyss,
spreading around my bones.

Even when the sheets pretend to hide
all the panic dilating my orbits.
A shroud of the horror
and your symphony of guttural is in the depths.

Verses born of the womb in complete sludge and wounds.
Cursed hair of the creature tried to strangle me.

Oh! There's a hell of scarlet veins on her eyes!
Penetrating sentence.
I can see the impurities, chaos and thousands of viscera
Take your eyes off the creature!

Your breath made of blasphemy and vipers came over to me.
The whole body exhales a smell of swamp.

Gradually, slides the disgusting nails
for the perimeters of my existence, stain the flesh
with a repulsive mouth, stole the ghost of my bowels,
terrible hunter of the souls and your clemency
in a delicate slowness, devoured the rests pulsating in my body.

At the end, fantastic banquet,
the creature evaporated and left a red trail in the moonlight.

~ Morphine Epiphany
Sao Paulo, Brazil

Green Monarch Leshy

Get It

2 Fresh Mint Leaves
1 large Kale Leaf
1 Kiwi, peeled
1 slice Seedless Watermelon
½ Peach, peeled
½ Mango, peeled
16 oz Vanilla Ice Cream

Mix It

1. Puree mint, kale, kiwi, watermelon, peach and mango.
2. Add vanilla ice cream and blend until smooth.

Read It

The leshy. What can I say? A bit of a loner if you ask me. Stays in the forest, no friends, all foe. Just try not to piss it off and you'll be fine. Maybe. Ya better make an extra shake just in case...

He, The Forest

The Leshy snickers when the lycanthrope shifts
from wolf to man, a quarter of an inch,
and chases the changeling down twisting paths
where the village signposts skew to a glade,
thwacked with the axe that drives pine above bone.

All winter he hunches in glimmer of boulder,
stroking the halted moss with the cratered
moons of his cheek until spring sprouts a beard,
and in chirping, shrinks; a peasant seizes
in laughter, rolls in the grass-blades tickling him dead.

Summer. Stay high in your tree stands, hunters.
The antlers that jut from the berries climb down
to visors of root over fireflies-eyes, a bark-gap
nose and scum-skimmed teeth of the river—
bed stones. The tree's a safe bet if it's let you alone.

And all you warming in autumn taverns,
watch for the glow in the whites of your cohorts,
watch that the cinders carom from the steins
hung in lines behind the bar to the eye, and watch
watch, watch and remember, no ember grows green—

If you ever wish to be seen again in your fauna
hued flesh. His step leads not home save for bones
of the lost. Green Monarch of forests, sticky
as hives, cool joints a'crackle like wood in a stove,
weaves wreaths of hoof-prints where ribcages grow.

~ Jay Outhier
New Jersey, USA

Caribbean Demon Passion

Get It

2 Passion Fruits
½ Guava
½ Pomegranate
1 pint Coconut Coconutmilk®
   Nondairy Frozen Dessert

Mix It

1. Use a high speed blender to puree pomegranate seeds.
2. Add passion fruit and guava and puree.
3. Blend with frozen non-dairy dessert until smooth.

Read It

Ooh, I just love glittery things. And love stories. Especially demon love stories. And caribbean drinks. So much passion...

We Are Legion

The sea glass and shell bracelet glitters on my wrist.

I see you choosing the pearly nautilus,
To twist together with the beer bottle green sliver;
A copper wire binding the two with a spiral
of Milky Way embellishment.

I loiter at your beach hut
Under the cool of a grove of palm trees,
At the edge of the Caribbean Sea.
Painted yellow and white:
the floorboards sandy, hanging chimes tinkling,
Your reclaimed treasures, offered with a smile,
Accompanied by the dulcet notes of your ukulele.
Your tawny horns hidden under a batik bandanna,
Sometimes your battered fisherman's hat.
Never seen by the undiscerning tourists,
Or the uninitiated locals.

I have seen you defend your kingdom with your brothers-in-arms,
Ripping and tearing, decapitating with your centuries old weapon,
Gore stained muscles rippling with exertion and exhilaration.
The warrior rage in your eyes
Matching the bloodlust in mine.

You fasten one last chip chip shell to the driftwood dream catcher.
It's almost teatime: the four o'clock sun streaming in,
The bits of glass sparkling.
I close the distance between us,
Free your sun-bleached locks, expose your exquisite curved horns.
I press my lips against yours, run my fingers through your hair…

The bracelet on my wrist glitters in the sun.

~ Allison Shepherd
Marabella, Trinidad and Tobago

HAIKU SHOTS

Hey, y'all! Who's up for shots? I mean proper shots with alcohol and all. Ya know, the kind that come in a cute little glass, not a syringe, of course.

Have one, have a couple or have one of each. Meet a few of our guests, their introductions are short but far from sweet.

Enjoy, y'all!

Haiku by Darkling

shrouded, crouched, veiled face
weeping, screaming, in the night
harbinger of doom

~ Machleif Cemetery

Screaming Banshee

3 oz vodka, 2 ½ oz peach schnapps, 2 ½ oz peach juice, 1 pkg unflavored gelatin, 1 slice jalapeño or ghost pepper ~ soak pepper in vodka, heat juice and gelatin until dissolved, add vodka and schnapps, pour into shot glasses; chill.

Haiku by JE Mason

manticore: deadly
its tail is known to poison
a beguiling grin

~ Illinois, USA

Manticore Poison

1 part kahlúa
1 part irish cream liqeuer
1 part amarretto

layer in shot glass

Haiku by Sarah Yasin

across midnight shores
trailing streams of opal slime
the sea-dragon slinks

~ Maine, USA

Sea-Dragon

1 part vodka
1 part blue curaçao
1 part lime juice

shake with ice and pour into
shot glasses

Haiku by Diane de Anda

he sprinkles the blood
across the white rose petals
a vampire romance

~ California, USA

Vampire Blood

1 part white tequila
1 part red curaçao

layer in a shot glass

Haiku by Vanessa Noel Graham

fingers through the sheets
heart pounding, push them away
too late—it has me

~ California, USA

Sweet Dreams

1 part root beer
1 part butterscotch schnapps

shake and pour

Haiku by Minerva Cerridwen

my long, sharp fingers
peel off your pretty faces
pop them like balloons

~ Vlaams-Brabant, Belgium

Balloon Poppers

1 part creme de banana
1 part strawberry schnapps
splash of kahlúa

shake, pour, and top with whipped
cream and a cherry

Haiku by Darkling

evil spirits lurk
peeking behind window eyes
cleaving to your soul

~ Machleif Cemetery

Dybbuk Possession

1 pkg black cherry gelatin, 8 oz
pomegranate juice, 8 oz kinky blue
~ dissolve gelatin in warm juice, mix in
cold kinky blue liqueur, pour into shot
glasses and chill.

PARTY PUNCH

What's a party without a big bowl of punch—with or without the alcohol spike? Not much of a party, at all if ya ask me.

Pour yourself a glass and meet the last of our guests. Y'all might want to pour an extra glass or two for these Beasties.

They're an eclectic bunch and like to get a bit wild. And some of them have been known to take things too far so don't drop your guard. Or your drink!

Enjoy, y'all!

The Drinks

Tortured Pirate Punch

Dragon's Claw Punch

Smokin' Zombie Punch

Green Goblin Punch

Vampire Champagne Punch

Goddess Blackberry Rum Punch

Cannabalistic Bourbon Punch

Violet Vampiress Punch

Dancing Revenant Punch

Sasquatch Mocha Punch

Deadly Sunset Punch

Enchanted Forest Punch

Tommy's Tappin' Graveyard Punch

Deadman's Swamp Punch

The Poetry

Torture of a Pirate by Ethan Nahte

Food Shopping by Anne M Gibson

Smoke-town Zombies by James Quinn

Just Put Out Your Hand by Juleigh Howard-Hobson

Hunger for Life: A Chant by Andrew Leon Hudson

My Parent's Don't Like Kali 'Cause She Drives a Mustang by Wolf Boy

Dinner with Jerry by Sally Max

Eventide by KA Opperman

Sodium-Vapor by Lisa Treece

When Monsters Share by Shawn Chang

Underneath the Red Moon by Linda M Crate

Siren of the Woods by Qurat Dar

Tommy's Knocking by Patrick Winters

New Fur for Old Skin by Oliver Smith

Tortured Pirate Punch

Get It

1 liter Jamaican Rum
2 liters Cherry Cola
1 jar Maraschino Cherries

Mix It

1. Pour rum and maraschino cherries, including juice, into a punch bowl.
2. Add cherry cola and ice; mix well.
3. Pour a glass, turn the pirate on your left and drink it down. Laugh mockingly as he begs for 'just a drop 'o grog, please!'

Read It

Ahoy, y'all! I sure wouldn't mind sailing the seven seas, plundering towns and collecting booty (wink, wink). Wait? Torture? Pirates never have pretty deaths, do they? Given a choice, I think I'd rather walk the plank straight to Davey Jones' locker. Y'all enjoy the punch but keep a weather eye open, matey...

Torture of a Pirate

Ravens pluck mine eyes
as demons pluck my soul.
Peck my heart from my chest—
Innards pulled the length of the gallows' pole.

My neck did not break
as the noose pulled raw and taut.
No quarter was I thus given
for I am a pirate, which they sought.

I dangle and choke, for air I wheeze.
Blood seeps through cuts from rocks thrown...
Sweat trickles and burns beneath the skin.
I long for my ship 'pon which I call home.

Death would be a mercy...
a boon greatly cherished,
but the gods seek vengeance,
so I linger, twist and perish.

~ Ethan Nahte
Arkansas, USA

Dragon's Claw Punch

Get It

2 parts Vodka

1 part Orange Liqueur

½ part Benedictine

4 parts Pomegranate Juice

4 parts Pineapple Juice

2 parts Apple Juice

1 part White Grape Juice

Sliced Lime

Pomegranate Seeds

Mix It

1. Pour all ingredients into a large punch bowl and mix well.
2. Add ice as desired.
3. Drop pomegranate seeds and lime slices on top.

Read It

Dragons are so misunderstood. Y'all think they pick random victims. Totally not the case. But still, ya never know what a dragon might take personally or who might be the next tasty meal. Just sayin', y'all might try being a little nicer.

Dragons do love spiciness...

Food Shopping

The parking lot's dimples retained last night's storm
each wheel well shimmering with rainbows
when the Cadillac rolled in, heavy.

I threw open the door and clambered out.
First sandals, then navy blue cotton pants
festooned with smiling crescent moons
then a linen shirt,
puffy sleeves stained with potions and charms
a beard that covered eyelet and drawstring close at the collar
A practiced motion tucked the point on the hat of a wizard point
under the door frame.
I was muttering even before I had the door closed.

The dragon pulled open one heavy emerald eyelid.

It was entirely too difficult to park these days, I thought,
with all these spots reserved for the undeserving.
"Reserved for expectant mothers"
Nobody asked them to get pregnant

"Reserved for parents with toddlers"
Nobody asked them to raise uncontrollable brats.
"Reserved for Naga"
Well, if the Naga don't want to cross the parking lot
they should take the bus, I thought.

The dragon rolled over and rested her head on the roof ledge
she pictured a naga slithering behind fifteen parked cars
on a Winter Solstice feast night
with drivers tearing in and out of the lot
The tallest Naga the dragon had ever met
wouldn't have been able to rest her chin
on the bumper of my Escalade.

She watched me carefully.

My volume rose as my muttering grew heated
each location an offense
Motorcycle parking
Aluminum bicycle racks whose peeling paint
exposed last year's colors
Plate metal broom stands impregnated with security spells
Thick wooden perches for Harpies and Vampire Bats

The dragon's scales shimmered in the sunlight
she rose onto her haunches
and dropped a few gold coins in a box for the purpose.

"Disabled parking! Lazy good-for-nothings!"
I spat
and then I spotted the Purple Claw on the back window
the mark of a warrior disabled battling a Leviathan.
Only the elite soldiers made it out of those campaigns alive.

I'd been attacked by a wyvern myself once
gathering spell components too close to a nest
Alone, injured, down to my last hundred gil
If it hadn't been for my charisma
Scamming that poor old woman out of her healing potions
Her livelihood
Well, she didn't really need the money, I figured.
I never thought about
How I'd make illuminated scrolls
Or my truck payment
Or dinner
had I not been lucky that day.

I thought "those people" get all the good spots in the lot.

And when the lieutenant in dress uniform
rolled her wheelchair to that car
arm still bandaged
left leg missing at the knee
I said, "Oh! A woman! Well no wonder you lost the fight!"

The dragon swooped off the roof
and plucked me off the tarmac
before the lieutenant could flip me the bird.

Tucked away in an enormous to-go bag
I screamed for help at ten thousand feet
and the dragon wondered if she still had antacids at home.

Spicy food was so tasty.

~ Anne E Gibson
Pennsylvania, USA

Smokin' Zombie Punch

Get It

Coconut Creme

Black Food Coloring

2 parts White Rum

2 parts Gold Rum

1 part 151-Proof Rum

1 part Triple Sec

2 parts Lemon Lime Soda

2 parts Ginger Ale

Mix It

1. Mix coconut cream and black food coloring until combined. Pour into ice cube trays and freeze overnight.

2. Mix rums, triple sec, soda and ginger ale in a large punch bowl.

3. Place black coconut ice cubes in glasses and pour punch over ice.

Read It

Are y'all prepared for a zombie invasion? No? I didn't think so. Listen, these zombies are no joke. Grab some punch—better get some to go too, you're gonna need to load up—and get ready to smoke some zombies...

Smoke-town Zombies

PART 1 ~ FRIDAY NIGHT

Friday night
Smoking Kush
Getting high
Shelby park

Friday night
With my nigga
No school
No worries

Friday night
In the park
Cracking up
With my nigga
. . . . .
Strange noises
sticks crackling
Someone coming
Weird noises
In the woods.

Let's go
Creepin in
Phone out
Gun out

Breathing, Breathing, Breathing
. . . . .
From the trees
Crazy Bitch!
Bloody mouths
Sharp yellow teeth
Jumps on a nigga
Man get the gun!

Blam! Blam!
First bitch down
Two more of them
Jump down the tree
Let's run!

Jumps on my nigga
Bites his neck
I run

My nigga screams
Slits his throat
Drinks his blood
I don't even know to use this gun
Oh shit!

Gotta get out
Drop my damn phone
Can't see
Make a call
Hopefully another one of those
mutherfuckas don't….

PART 2 ~ RECOVERY

Neck hurts
Drowsy
Mouth dry
I cry
In my bed
….my nigga dead..
My nigga dead…
My nigga dead…
My nigga dead…

PART 3 ~ TRANSFORMATION

Setting: Mirror
Dark spots on skin
Eyes turning yellow
Fingernails growing
Hair growing longer and longer
Speech slurring and slurring
Strength increasing by minutes
Temperature getting colder and colder
Skin getting browner and browner
And why do I feel the need to
Kill and eat everyone downstairs?!?
I'll kill all of you!!! I'll kill you all!!!

PART 4 ~ LAST BOW

Losing myself;
Can't remember:
The time I was eight
My favorite birthday cake
My mom's brown eyes
My dad's shirt and tie

All gone
My favorite sport
My first kiss
My middle name
My first and last

All gone
My mother; at her throat
My father; ripped his spine
My sister; ate her brains

My father's gun
My father's gun

Last option
Last…option

Click! Blam!

~ James Quinn
Kentucky, USA

Green Goblin Punch

Get It

2 parts Vodka
1 part Blue Curaçao
1 part Pineapple Juice
1 part Pear Juice
1 part White Grape Juice
3 parts Lemon-Lime soda
Lemon and Lime Slices

Mix It

1. Mix all ingredients in a large punch bowl.
2. Garnish with fresh lime and lemon.

Read It

Never trust a goblin. They'll steal your children before you can blink. Ya know, unless you're tired of the noisy brat. Than by all means, leave that window open. Just a crack will do...

Just Put Out Your Hand

We can take you out past the shadows,
where paths that do not look like paths
all lead.

Winding ....wending....
down around thick roots and twisted stems,
far beyond here.

We don't care that you're a child,
we don't mind,
all you need to do is reach.

Just put out your hand
and let us take it,
we can take you places that you'll love.

Sure, you can go home,
anytime,
we promise.

Leave your window open just a crack tonight,
we'll slip through when the moon is high
and take you to roam the hollow hills.

All within a stone's throw
of your hand,
once you take one of ours in it.

Fairies dance in sacred circles,
wild folk surround each meadow and each wood,
the forest is alive with spirits.

Kin of ours,
each one forbidden to take a child,
except for us.

Tell no one. Understood?

~ Juleigh Howard-Hobson
Washington, USA

Vampire Champagne Punch

Get It

2 bottles Champagne
2 liters Raspberry Ginger Ale
2 quarts Lime Sherbet
1 pint Raspberry Sorbet
½ pint Fresh Raspberries

Mix It

1. Slightly melt lime sherbet. Mix with champagne and ginger ale.
2. Top with scoops of raspberry sorbet and fresh raspberries.

Read It

Nothing like a little champagne to tame the hunger pains. Okay, I know. If you're a vampire, it's not as good as blood. It is, however, terrifically sweet and bubbly. Fresh raspberries mixed with champagne are the perfect combination to keep that youthful flavor, I mean appearance...

Hunger For Life

I hear the call, and come to eat you all.
I love the sound: it leads to where you're found,
All night, all day, it beats your life away.
So you are doomed, though it goes unconsumed
Because all flesh is fresh,
The heart apart.

My heart is dry, each beat a dusty sigh.
My touch is cold, like other things so old
That time forgot—yet such as you burn hot
With youthful life! My hunger's like a knife
For what your veins contain!
The blood is good.

I sense the warm, and sense myself deform,
Each of my teeth a blade drawn from its sheath.
You try to hide—I'm not to be denied,
Oh tiny thing! You sound the heart-bell's ring!
I smell how thin your skin,
How sweet your meat!

Wise creatures flee when they lay eyes on me.
Instead... you stand, though your death is at hand.
You're young, it's true—but youth fuels hungers too,
And I scent rage, that flavour lost with age.
You meet my gaze unfazed,
Though fear lurks near.

My pantomime of life seems real this time…
Shall even I inevitably die?
What once felt lust, transformed from flesh to dust?
…if so, advance! I'll join your mortal dance!
From fatal blows, blood flows--
One gives, one lives!

~ Andrew Leon Hudson
Madrid, Spain

Goddess Blackberry Rum Punch

Get It

1 part Vodka

1 part Spiced Rum

8 parts Blackberry Ginger Ale

½ part Lime Juice

Fresh Blackberries

Fresh Lime slices

Mix It

1. Mix vodka, rum, ginger ale and lime juice in a large punch bowl.
2. Garnish with fresh blackberries lime slices.

Read It

Ya know, when I was alive, all the good girls wanted to date the bad boys. They were dangerous and exciting and had cool, flashy cars. Oh, the best part? The parents hated it! And sometimes, good boys loved bad girls. I mean, who wouldn't want to date a kick-ass goddess with a Mustang? This blackberry rum punch will help bring out your inner bad girl or bad boy. It might even attract a few...

My Parents Don't Like Kali 'Cause She Drives a Mustang

My parents don't approve of Kali

'cause she pulls up at our house in a shiny black mustang with flames on the sides

blasting punk from the souped-up speakers that line the insides.

She grins and flashes the peace sign at my mom

when I come out in my dorky hoodie, nervous and flushed,

and she pulls distractedly at the left shoulder strap of her black tank

while two more hands light up a half-smoked Camel.

"I wish she wouldn't do that in front of the house,"

Mom whispers tersely, but I ignore her.

Kali pecks me ferociously

and waves bye at mom's back while I hop in.

We speed all the way to the arcade,

and all the way she's daring me to give her road head

and sipping from a brown bag jammed awkwardly into the cup holder

in between the driver's seat and shotgun.

We hurtle into the parking lot,

riding up on the curb with one wheel on the way in,

and she jerks the car into park, bites me on the shoulder

and grins saucily.

"You ready to get your ass whipped in Tekken 3 or what."

I laugh, and blush, and she slings an arm around my shoulder

and, five rounds of Tekken later,

when I finally complain that it isn't fair because she's got six hands,

she lets go with all but two, flips me the double birds with two more,

fixes her hair with a fifth, and uses her last to tip the brown bag to her mouth,

leaving black lipstick stains on the lip of the bottle.

The other teenagers gather round,

staring in stupefied awe 'cause she knows all the combo moves,

and she rattles them off with an elegant ruthlessness,

ripping out my character's spine for the finisher.

"HAH!" She crows, slamming the brown bag down onto the console,

"that's six in a row. You owe me road head, bitch."

I blush a darker shade of maroon,

and this gawking kid with thick glasses trembles

as he asks for her autograph. She laughs, takes the cap off her lipstick,

and scrawls a heart next to her name on his right lens,

and as she takes a long smoke break in the alley behind the arcade,

some hefty dude with tats all over his forearms

stumbles past on his way out of the bar a couple blocks down

"Hey, pretty lady," he leers,

"I wonder what you've got on under that—"

You can't even see her move.

He drops, headless, and the first thing out of my mouth

after half a minute of stunned silence is

"Dude! Where did you get a samurai sword?!
Like where did that even come from?!"
She raises an eyebrow.
"Bitch, I'm a goddess! Whatever."
She sticks the blade in his gut,
twisting it as she makes a face. "Ugh.
These guys are all gristle.
I won't even be able to doggy bag this."
She pauses, frowning.
"His heart smells okay, though.
Give me a second—"
and she bends down
and yeah
I almost vomit when she asks if I want any.
She licks her fingers,
dumps the rest in her trunk,
and drives us to the bayou.
As he sinks with unsettling quiet, she giggles
and tugs at a shoulder strap
with another arm slung around my shoulder
another still holding the bag
two more trying to undo my belt,
"Jesus, Kali,
here?! Are you nuts?!"
She tilts back her head and laughs

and blood runs down her neck

"Fine. But you still owe me road head."

Well, I do my best to deliver on that

and she pecks me again when we pull up at the curb

in front of my place. "Well," she croons,

"I hope you had fun. I did."

I tug at my collar. "Yeah, that was great.

But, um, like, next time,

like, could you not kill anybody?"

She shrugs.

"I'll do my best.

Sweet dreams."

And she's off in a spray of black exhaust,

and I sneak upstairs past my parents' bedroom

so they won't wake up, see the time, and flip.

I flop down on my mattress

"God, what a mad woman

I think I'm in love,"

and my dreams are filled with headless dudes

and ass-kicking Tekken combos and samurai swords

and the moonlight on Kali's teeth

as her neck glistens like black bayou water.

~ Wolf Boy
Colorado, USA

Cannabalistic Bourbon Punch

Get It

Fresh Bing Cherries, halved
Ground Cardamom
Raw Sugar
4 parts Orange Jjuice
3 parts Cherry Liqueur
2 parts Bourbon
1 part Grenadine
4 parts Club Soda

Mix It

1. Coat cherries with cardamom; spread evenly on a baking sheet. Roast in 325° F oven for 20 minutes; cool.

2. Sprinkle raw sugar and roasted cherries in the bottom of a punch bowl. Add orange juice; gently mash to blend.

3. Mix cherry liqueur, bourbon and grenadine; mix well with orange juice.

4. Top with club soda and serve over ice.

Read It

Ooh, a dinner party! Y'all are in for a real treat. Unless your name's Jerry. I'm so glad this isn't a first date...

Dinner With Jerry

My first time cooking for my new boyfriend.
A romantic dinner to win his heart.
Hugs and kisses to start a great weekend.
"I'm sorry, my love, you can't see this part."

A chop, a blend, a dice, a cadaver.
Seasoned with garlic, and bubbly brown.
The lungs, the heart, the sweet meats, the bladder.
Homemade sangria to wash it all down.

The table is set, the candles are lit.
Oh, what have I done? Do I dare reveal?
"Tasty!" He proclaims, "I really love it!
What is this beef? No, it must be some veal."

I smile, proud of my skills, and my surprise.
"That jerk Jerry from work met his demise."

~ Sally Max
Florida, USA

Violet Vampiress Punch

Get It

1 part Raspberry Lemonade
2 parts Blackberry Ginger Ale
Raspberry Sherbet
Fresh or Frozen Raspberries
Fresh or Frozen Blackberries

Mix It

1. Mix lemonade and ginger ale.
2. Add scoops of raspberry sherbet and mix lightly.
3. Top with whole raspberries and blackberries.

Read It

Beware, young men, if a beautiful girl asks you for a drink. She might have something a little different in mind than a boring beer in a red solo cup. Something more like a living vein. This punch doesn't come from a beating heart, but the violet crimson liquid is to die for...

Eventide

When violet turns the eventide
A revenant is seen to glide
Along the haunted woodland wide,
Diaphanous and pale.

The silver stars of even crown
The ghostly tulle that serves to gown
Her body from the brow and down,
Bare curves beneath the veil.

The bats attend her silken train,
And hover round her raven mane.
She hungers for a living vein
On life blood's beating trail.

When violet turns the eventide,
Beware the crimson-mouthèd bride,
For many men have gladly died
To fill her sanguine grail.

~ KA Opperman
California, USA

Dancing Revenant Punch

Get It

3 qts Crushed Ice

3qts Lemonade

12 oz White Grape Juice
Concentrate

1 Lemon, thinly sliced

1 Cucumber, thinly sliced

Mix It

1. .Mix ice, lemonade and grape juice concentrate in punch bowl.
2. Float sliced lemon and cucumber on top.

Read It

Y'all always say you'll sleep when you're dead. Sorry to disappoint you, but that's not usually how it works. Ever hear of the restless dead? That's probably much closer to the truth. Me? Nah, I'm not restless. Even though I'm dead. And I don't sleep much. But I do love to dance...

Sodium-Vapor

The light of the night is sulfur.
Orange and rotten flame.
She dances with her head just so—
an awkward angle on her breast.
Eyes a lifeless black and yellow.
Tongue a fat and swollen larvae,
slithering over cracked lips.
Hips like a carousel,
swivel and swerve,
to a long forgotten rhythm—
no longer in her chest.

~ Lisa Treece
Michigan, USA

Sasquatch Mocha Punch

Get It

- 2 pots Brewed Coffee, double strength
- 2 pkgs Hot Cocoa Mix
- 1 pint Vanilla Ice Cream
- 1 pint Chocolate Ice Cream

Mix It

1. Add cocoa to hot brewed coffee, mix and cool with an equal amount of ice.
2. Pour into a punch bowl; add scoops of vanilla and chocolate ice cream.
3. Mix to slightly melt and serve.

Read It

Y'all know what's worse than being eaten by a monster? Being eaten by two. But, hey, sharing is caring. If y'all don't want to fall prey to these big, bad Beasties, ya better make a large batch of this mocha punch and share. Come on now, y'all. There's enough ice cream here for everyone...

When Monsters Share

Souvenirs fresh from the wild
still writhing on display as
her forked tongue twitches
and his tail whisks briskly
in pride; partners in crime
with her behind the scenes
and him undertaking the labor
of delivery. It is his
custom to finish exploring
on his hunting grounds
before dawn and hers
to pleasantly bide her time
by the window, expecting his
return—often characterized by his
manner of dragging mangled pieces
of carcasses beyond identification
to the equally customary potlucks
for two. She always executes
her first move by sinking
her fangs into the prey,

enjoying the texture of soft fur,

finishing masterfully by devouring

the carrion whole, dissolved in

her acid; his tongue lolling, he drives

his claws into necks, liberally

spilling blood onto glass. And

whenever both become too surfeited

to continue dining, he moves

the remains closer delicately

to the window—paws still

glistening in the moonlight

with wet blood—and tosses

the mutilated bodies one after

the other out via defenestration

to the mercy of their

homeless starving canine pals

prowling in wait below.

~ Shawn Chang
British Columbia, Canada

Deadly Sunset Punch

Get It

1 part Lemonade or Limeade

2 parts Apple Cranberry Juice

2 parts Pear Juice

2 parts Sparkling Mineral Water

Fresh Cranberries

Mix It

1. Mix lemonade, apple-cranberry juice and pear juice in a large punch bowl.
2. Slowy add sparkling mineral water.
3. Float cranberries on top.

Read It

If y'all never seen a blood moon, ya really should. At least once in your life. I mean, they're pretty cool when you're dead too, but it's just not the same. Dancing and singing in a field of wildflowers beneath marshmallow clouds and a deep, dark blood red moon. So invigorating! Ya never know what awaits...

Underneath the Red Moon

Beneath a blood red moon
stiff and motionless
a body
waits to be found
her lips like spring flowers
bruised by frost
purple and red dance together
a deadly sunset in the milk white
of clouds,
blue eyes gazing forever into an eternity
none living have ever seen;
blonde hair like goldenrod upon the wet grass—
two puncture wounds in her throat
from a creature none would
care to admit exists
except for in literature and nightmares,
but they would be wrong;
her eyes hold the terror that they'll never admit to,
"vampyre"

her eyes shriek forever and forever
as they say amen in a church a few feet away—
she waits patiently
for the dead have all the time in the world
to be found beneath the hungry lips of the moon,
and she knows perhaps one of her friends
will join her in this death hand clasp because the beast's
hunger would not be sated by her blood alone.

~ Linda M Crate
Pennsylvania, USA

Enchanted Forest Punch

Get It

3 parts Sparkling Mineral Water
3 parts Pomegranate Juice
1 part Elderberry Syrup
½ part Fresh Lime Juice
Fresh Rosemary Sprigs
Fresh Mint Leaves
Fresh Blackberries
Fresh Cranberries

Mix It

1. Pour the sparkling mineral water, pomegranate juice, elderberry syrup and lime juice into a punch bowl.
2. Stir in the blackberries, cranberries, mint leaves and rosemary sprigs.
3. Serve over ice.

Read It

Y'all keep going out in the woods alone. How many times do I have to warn you? Never trust a beautiful stranger, especially one leading you deeper into the woods. Fairies are gorgeous creatures—some of my best friends are fairies—but we're not living in a fairytale here...

Siren of the Woods

All tinkling laughs and muted lights
She dances,
Feet barely touching
The ground,
The forest going silent to watch.
She is a haze, the glow from an oil lamp,
The setting sun made flesh—
Flaring and flickering as she weaves through the trees,
Invariably being followed by some new admirer
Foolish enough to wander by the woods
Without bread or iron in his pockets,
Consumed by her smoldering eyes
And too bewitched
To break free from her hold,
Her newest plaything, to be taunted
Until dark, led into those unholy worlds
Where the stars and moon have been swallowed up,
And nothing lives,
To the same fate as countless others
Taken by the
Siren of the woods.

~ Qurat Dar
Ontario, Canada

Tommy's Tappin' Graveyard Punch

Get It

1 part Grape Juice
1 part Orange Soda
1 part Lemon Lime Soda
1 part Ginger Ale
Ice Glove

Mix It

1. Fill a latex glove (or two) with water and freeze overnight.
2. Combine grape juice, sodas and ginger ale in a punch bowl.
3. Chill with ice glove in the center of the punch bowl.

Read It

See, here's the problem. Y'all are so worried about what happens after ya die and what it's like on the other side that ya forget how to live while you're still alive. I can't tell ya what it's like, no one can. It's a rather personal thing. One thing I do know—nothin good ever came from the living trying to find out...

Tommy's Knockin'

We wondered about death,
My brother and I—
Of what, if anything,
Lay beyond our life.
Would we drift like sweet slumber?
Or ascend to a Heaven?
Or would we float, float, float
Through the days and nights?

"Comes something," said he,
"Comes nothing," said I,
And nothing would
Persuade me otherwise.
"Then let's visit the Tommyknockers,"
My brother said then,
"Where they knock, knock, knock
In the old Marsden Mines."

So, we snuck out that night
With our lanterns in hand,
Treading the forest

Beneath the moon's band,
'Til we reached on old shaft—
A mouth stretching deep
Down into the dark, dark, dark
Heart of the land.

We waited a good while,
My doubts still true—
Until we heard a tapping
Coming through the gloom.
"See!" cried my brother,
And how he did dance—
When earth shook, shook, shook,
And fell down like doom.

I survived the matter,
Though my brother did not,
And now I stand above him
At a well-chosen spot.
And my blood is chilled,
Looking down at the coffin:
For there's a knock, knock, knocking
Down there with his rot.

~ Patrick Winters
Illinois, USA

Deadman's Swamp Punch

Get It

10 parts Peach Juice

1 part Pineapple Juice

1 part Cran Raspberry Juice

1 part Apple Juice

1 part Grape Juice

2 parts Coconut Cream

2 parts Coconut Water

1 part Rose Water

Sprinkle of cinnamon

Mix It

1. Mix juices in a large punch bowl.

2. In a separate bowl, combine coconut cream, coconut water and rose water.

3. Add mixture to punch bowl and stir.

4. Sprinkle with cinnamon.

Read It

Go join the circus, they said. It'll be fun, they said. Y'all go right on ahead and do whatever ya want. Me? I'm perfectly content watching the clowns and Wolfmaster when they pass through the valley. They do put on a spectacular show...

New Fur for Old Skin

A sweet song rose in subtle flood
To call the village to the fair:
Where Lamia sang so sweetly,
Dancing in the midnight mire,
And white ghosts floated in the air.

All the would-be wolves and lovers
Rushed from their woodland bowers,
Intent on the charms of darkly
handsome demon, sighing siren,
serpent girls; priapic satyrs

And the cherry-lips of vampires.

The priest prayed hard and long
To banish these wicked spectral things
By the exercise of discipline,
Through sermons and mournful hymns

Served on Sundays as long as life,
As cold as death, and twice as grim.
But under the glowing pumpkin-moon

He saw his congregation feast ,
And prance around the midnight fire

To pipes and flutes and wild drum beats,
Where a circus grew on painted poles

Like a mushroom in the midnight soil.
It swelled its tents like autumn fruit,
That ripened by the orchard wall.

The canvas split and spilled a crowd
Of clowns; a carnival of freaks:
Bareback riders, fortune tellers,
Monsters, nightmares, trick shots, tumblers
jugglers, fakirs, and candy sellers,

Who paraded down the village street
Meandering like the minds of fools
From Deadman's Swamp to churchyard gate,

Over the humpback bridge to meet
The Wolfmaster down at the mill-pond pool...

"A thousand years man and monster,
Have I pitched my circus here;
Watched you build the bustling town
And all grow very sad and old
And miserably austere.

I bring all the pleasures your life denies;
All the wild, fantastic things;
 Things that fairy-tales left behind."
The priest bent his back and fled away,

But the Wolfmaster ran beside.

"So many sights you'll see," he said,
"The stars that bleed, the flesh that sighs,
The heart of Sagittarius that beats
So blackley in the starry sky."
The Wolfmaster reached inside his coat

And gave the priest a new wolf face,
And free along the road he raced
After fuller moons, and purer snows;
In search of worlds of wild desire
In deeper woods where bright blood flows.

~ Oliver Smith
Gloucestershire, UK

©Cooney

Hey, which one of y'all invited the clowns? Come on now, y'all should know better. They can be real party crashers.

Haven't you ever been to a carnival, seen a parade, gone to the fair, hosted a children's party—watched IT?

Well, it's a little late to think about that now, don't ya think? They're here and they want to party.

These next drinks and treats should keep them happy for a while, just as long as that Pennywise dude doesn't show up again.

Speaking of Pennywise, did y'all see that movie? Supposed to be based on a book written by some guy named King. September 1986, I'm told.

Ya know, they released that movie in September and there's a sequel, a year later—also in September.

I think that King guy's birthday is in September too.

Hmm. I wonder what's so special about September? No matter. Here in the Machleif Cemetery, every day you're alive is a birthday!

Happy Birthday, Stephen King. The clowns have come out to play.

Enjoy, y'all!

CLOWN POEMS AND TREATS

Clown Night by LS Reinholt

Within the Darkness of the Carnivale by Donald Armfield

Friend or FOEccacia Bread Sticks

Chocolate Cherry Killer Clown Shake

Colorful Clown Smoothie

Deceptively Sweet Clown Tea

Red Harlequin Party Punch

Balloon Popping Cinnamon Marshmallow Coffee

Evil Jester Cheesecake

Clown Night

I've got my gloves
I've got my shoes
The makeup's on my face.
Come to me friends
Come run with me
It's time to start the chase.
The clowns will play tonight.

The little boys
The little girls
And mums and daddies too
All try to run
And then to hide
We'll search the whole town through.
The clowns will hunt tonight.

By moon and stars
Through streets and parks
We'll search and play and call
Where will you hide?
Where can you run?
Too soon we'll find you all.
The clowns will feast tonight.

~ LS Reinholt
Ryomgard, Denmark

Friend or FOEccacia Bread Sticks

Get It

12 oz All-Purpose Flour, sifted
½ Tbsp Quick Rise Yeast
½ tsp Salt
½ tsp Sugar
½ tsp Garlic Powder
½ tsp Oregano
½ tsp Thyme

¼ tsp Rosemary
¼ tsp Basil
Dash Black Pepper
½ Tbsp Olive Oil
4 oz Warm Water
1 Tbsp Olive Oil
1 Tbsp Parmesan Cheese
5 oz Mozzarella Cheese

Mix It

1. Sift flour into a medium bowl. Add yeast, salt, sugar, garlic powder, oregano, thyme, rosemary, basil and pepper. Mix until well combined.
2. Knead in ½ Tbsp olive oil and warm water. Continue kneading on a lightly floured countertop, 5 to 8 minutes ot until smooth and elastic.
3. Lightly coat dough with oil, place in a clean bowl and cover with a damp cloth; let dough rest and rise for 20 minutes.

4. Finely grate parmesan and mozzarella cheese and combine, set aside.

5. Lightly grease an 8-inch baking sheet with oil or shortening.

6. Punch down dough and place on center of baking sheet; pat it down into a half-inch thick square.

7. Gently cut into 1-inch strips and cover with 1 Tbsp olive oil.

8. Sprinkle evenly with cheese mixture.

9. Bake at 350° F for 15 minutes or until golden brown.

10. Serve warm and share.

Read It

Ya know what clowns love? Carbs. They just can't help themselves—breads, doughnuts, cakes, pies, cookies, pastries of all kinds. These breadsticks will help keep the clowns in your life laughing and feasting on cheesy goodness. Ya know, instead of feasting on the neighbors. Speaking of neighbors—if y'all want to make friends with the new neighbors (or keep the old neighbors from calling the cops every time they hear a scream in the basement), bake an extra batch or two and take them over as a peace offering. Unless they're gluten-free. Please don't kill your neighbors. Just use a gluten-free flour instead.

Chocolate Cherry Killer Clown Shake

Get It

4 scoops Vanilla Ice Cream
Handful Milk Chocolate Chips
Cherry Sauce or Syrup
Maraschino Cherry

Mix It

1. Mix ice cream and chocolate chips in a blender until chocolate chips break into smaller pieces.
2. Drizzle cherry sauce down the sides of a clear glass.
3. Pour milkshake into glass and top with extra chocolate chips. Drizzle with cherry sauce and top with cherry.

Read It

I scream, you scream, the clowns scream for ice cream! If y'all love chocolate covered cherries, you're gonna love this too. The clowns love milkshakes and this one seems to be a favorite. Dare I say it? This one is to die for.

Colorful Clown Smoothie

Get It

8 oz Ice
2 Tbsp Greek Yoghurt
1 Tbsp honey
4 oz Blueberries
4 oz Raspberries
½ Mango

Mix It

1. Add all ingredients to a blender and blend on high until smooth.
2. Pour into a glass and enjoy!

Read It

If y'all decide to stay inside on Clown Night—maybe a wise choice—mix up one of these luscious fruit smoothies and crank up the music or watch a good horror flick. These colorful fruits make a delicious combination and the blender makes just enough noise to drown out the screams coming from somewhere inside.

Deceptively Sweet Clown Tea

Get It

4 bags Orange Tea
8 oz Granulated Sugar
1 qt Pineapple Juice

Mix It

1. Bring one quart water to a gentle boil; steep tea bags for 10 minutes.
2. Remove tea bags and stir in sugar.
3. Add pineapple juice and chill before serving over ice.

Read It

Clown Night can be so exhausting. This tea is a good pick-me-up and a perfect distraction from the mess going on outside. It's equally good served cold on hot days for cleaning up the neighborhood and served hot on cold nights when the wind—just keep telling yourself it's the wind—howls and ya need to stay alert.

Red Harlequin Party Punch

Get It

1 can Fruit Punch Energy Drink
1 qt Cranberry Juice
1 bottle Non-Alcoholic Moscato
Mixed Berries (fresh or frozen)
Lime
Sugar

Mix It

1. Mix energy drink, cranberry juice and non-alcoholic Moscato in a punch bowl.
2. Add mixed berries.
3. Rub rims of glasses with fresh lime and dip in sugar to coat before serving.

Read It

What's sadder than a Harlequin? A party without a bowl of punch. Don't worry, you won't get wasted drinking this one. It's alcohol-free but delivers quite a kick. This one will keep you on your toes all night.

Balloon Popping Cinnamon Marshmallow Coffee

Get It

16 oz Dark Roast Cold Brew
1 large Marshmallow
Red Hots® Cinnamon Candies
Half-and-Half
Whipped Cream
Red Sugar Sprinkles

Mix It

1. Add a few cinnamon candy pieces to the bottom of a glass; fill with cold brew coffee.
2. Drizzle the top with half-and-half; top with whipped cream and red sprinkles.
3. Insert 2-3 cinnamon candies into center of marshmallow. Place on top of whipped cream and enjoy!

Read It

Wow, that's a mouthful, isn't it? And a delicious mouthful at that. This coffee has just the right amount of sweet and spice to make your cares just float away. But seriously, don't believe anything those clowns say and never accept the red balloon.
Not everyone floats, ya know.

Evil Jester Cheesecake

Get It

For the Crust:
12 oz Almond Meal
3 Tbsp Dark Brown Sugar
6 Tbsp Butter

For the Cheesecake:
24 oz Cream Cheese, room temp
3 Eggs, room temp
6 oz Confectioner's Sugar
1 Tbsp Bourbon Vanilla Extract
3 oz Dark Chocolate Sauce

Mix It

1. Line a muffin pan with individual papers and preheat oven to 350° F. Place a bowl of water on bottom rack of oven.
2. Blend almond meal and brown sugar in a small bowl. Add melted butter and mix until well coated. Press approximately 1 Tbsp into each lined muffin cup and set aside.
3. Mix cream cheese on high speed until light and fluffy. Add eggs, one at a time, and mix until creamy. Add confectioner's sugar and vanilla and blend on low to medium speed until smooth.
4. Separate a fourth of the mixture into another bowl and stir in dark chocolate sauce.

5. Fill each muffin cup 2/3 full with plain cheesecake mix, top with 1 Tbsp chocolate cheesecake mix.
6. Use a toothpick to gently swirl chocolate into top half of each muffin cup.
7. Bake on center rack of oven for 20 to 25 minutes. Do not over-bake. Top, center will be soft but firm to the touch, sides will start to pull away when done.
8. Allow to cool to room temperature then refrigerate.

Read It

Clowns love desserts and I love cheesecake so this is the perfect treat to conclude Clown Night. Unlike some cheesecakes, these little jester cakes are much more forgiving if you slip up. So, y'all don't worry if ya never made a cheesecake before. Remember what I said about neighbors? And making friends? Whip up several of these to drop off to everyone in the neighborhood—the ones who survived Clown Night, that is. While you're at it, make several more for the clowns. They make amazing thank you gifts. I mean, they did let you live, right?

Within the Darkness of the Carnivále

I told my cousin the
Carnivále was in town
His eyes exhibited
fear, dread, a hidden
macabre that yield warning
and he instantly locked the doors
rocking back and forth.

I left him at the house
with his daunting fright
crying and begging me
to stay away from
the fairgrounds
failing to take heed
of his warning: I should've stayed...

Now my reflection shows
a chromatic horizon behind me
as if the lights never went dim over the Carnivále.
Even my shadow has a dancing

silhouette of the big top's pitch
and its twirling designs,
like an active halo displaying my art.

The grease paint absorbed into my pores and
branded my skin with a forever delightful-dread.
I imagine sutures or wires,
pinching the length of my spinal column
holding the suit in place
a colorful wardrobe that rises attention,
as I wave happily from afar...

It's too late to see the evil, that hides behind
my painted happiness and spectrum of gesture:
the laughter pulls you near,
closer and closer
as you approach me for the last time
and disappear into the darkness,
the darkness within the Carnivále.

~ Donald Armfield
Massachusetts, USA

Whew! All you Beasties and Ghouls sure do know how to party! I didn't think some of y'all were going to make it out of there alive, yet here you are.

Safe and sound at the break of day. When the sun's on the rise, the most monstrous of our guests drift back into the dark cool forest, head for their grave cave or vanish into the mist.

As for me, I'll be around the Machleif Cemetery, sharing the tales of the damned—living and deceased—while conjuring up some more treats for y'all. Werewolf Biscuits. Vampire Bites. Maybe a few other goodies too.

And who knows, maybe someday I'll get out of this cemetery for a while. See the world, do a little fright-seeing.

Don't worry, I'll send a postcard or three.

See ya around the valley!

~ Darkling

Congratulations to our contest winners:

Donald Armfield	Ashley Dioses	JoAnne Russell
Anton Cancre	Jill Hand	Alan Sessler
Shawn Chang	Carl Jennings	Lucy Snyder
	LS Reinholt	

And thank you to everyone who participated in
Darkling's Facebook Party:

Donald Armfield	John Linwood Grant
Anton Cancre	Minerva Cerridwen
Shawn Chang	Jill Hand
Ashley Dioses	Mathias Jansson
Vanessa Noel Graham	LS Reinholt

Rie Sheridan Rose
JoAnne Russell
Alan Sessler
Lucy Snyder

Special thanks goes out to Shawn Chang, Lycan
Valley's Recipe Rockstar, for his enthusiasm and
participation in Lycan Valley events.

Drink and Poem Quick Reference Guide

Each drink and corresponding poem is listed here by category in order of appearance. Drinks marked with an * contain alcohol; all others are non-alcoholic. With the exception of Cocktails/Mixed Drinks and Haiku Shots, nearly every recipe can be made non-alcoholic simply by removing the alcohol .

COFFEE AND TEA

*Monster Mash ~ The Monster Mash by John C Mannone
*Red Velvet Morning ~ The Morning Named Apollo: A Chimeric Blood Song by Stephanie Wytovich
*Full Moon Transformation ~ The Lycanthrope by Paula Berman
*Chocolate Amaretto Wendigo ~ The Hunter by EM Eastick
Butterscotch Night Owl ~ The Eyes by Mark Mihalko
Enchanted Faerie ~ Fated to Die by Sara Tantlinger
Black Dog Mocha ~ With Bared Teeth by Javier Gómez
Vampire and Cream Macchiato ~ In Our Past Mortality by Jay Rohr
Sweet & Spicy Werewolf Mocha ~ Lust in the Full Moon by Khalil Goddard
Wendigo Pumpkin Pie ~ Frontier Winter by CJ Thompson
Cinnamon Ginger Gargoyle ~ Evolution of a Young Lover by Frank Heather
*Undead Blackberry Brandy ~ Nosferatu by Michael H Hanson
Redcap Zinger ~ Redcap by Kurt Newton
*Whispering Moonlight Tea ~ The Night Whispers by Sarah Cannavo
Lost Princess ~ A Witch Reflects on Loss by Rie Sheridan Rose
Iced Brazilian Cha Mate ~ Backwards Footprints by Donald Armfield
Scottish Kelpie Secret Tea ~ Secrets of the Loch by JR Bournville
Luring Temptation Tea ~ A Siren's Pursuer by Donald Armfield
Wild Werewolf Chai ~ Hunger by Candace Robinson
Strawberry Rooibos Soul Eater ~ The Novealla of Vuorwro (#6) by Ron Riekki
Chimera Freedom Green Tea ~ Figment Fantastica by Taye Carroll

COCKTAILS AND MIXED DRINKS

*The Kraken ~ The Seafloor God by Ethan Hedman
*Blue Lagoon ~ A Kelpie's Promise by Trisha Wooldridge
*Lost At Sea ~ Siren's Song by LS Reinholt
*Black Widow ~ Widow's Weeds by Linda Lee Ruzicka
*Cherry Wine Disguise ~ Skin Walking by MF Senger
*Thieving Fairy ~ Stolen by Jillian Bost
*Goblin Sedator ~ Bedtime by Lynne Sargent
*Bruja Potion ~ The Witches Give Birth by Joshua Lupardus
*Spirit Bloom ~ The Rattling Tree by Rob E Boley
*Frozen Bloody Vampire ~ The Confession by Timothy Tarkelly
*Lambton Worm ~ An' I'd Swally the Little Bairns by Kimberly Brannon
*Zombie Tamer ~ Plague Ship by Emerian Rich
*Rural Hag ~ Death by Breaths by Gerri Leen
*Monster Metaphor ~ Eternal Epitaph by Don Campbell

SMOOTHIES

The Four Horsemen ~ And They Ride by Shana Scott
Faceless Yōkai ~ Noppera-bō by Samantha Lienhard
Blackened Night Sky ~ Black Vampire by Lavel Wideman
Magical Rebirth ~ The War Witch by SL Edwards
Full Mango Moon ~ The Power of the Moon by Ashley Dioses
The Siren Goddess ~ Fisherman's Lure by Ken MacGregor
Wendigo's Reflection ~ The Beast I Am by Jyothika Aaryan

MILKSHAKES

*The Drowned Devil ~ The Scab That Oozes by Nick Manzolillo
*Flaming Night Mare ~ Nightmare Upon Dissolution by Jason Ellis
*Wandering Gargoyle ~ Night On The Town by Andrew Dunlop
*Blackberry Faerie ~ The Faerie Rules by MJ Mars

The Frozen Imp ~ A Prank Too Far by Anne E Johnson
*Grinning Werewolf ~ Whitechapel by Samantha Potts
Mermaid Matcha & Cream ~ An Vorvoren a Senar by Darren Lester
Woven Silk Spider Egg ~ Frankenspider by Minerva Cerridwen
Türk Vampir Kahvesi ~ The Vampire Ogrencisi by Shalom Aranas
Cernunnos' Wild Hunt ~ Antlered Avenger by Kimmy Alan
Guardian of the Forest ~ Feetures by Shawn Chang
Seductive Succubus ~ Moon in Purple by Morphine Epiphany
Green Monarch Leshy ~ He, The Forest by Jay Outhier
Caribbean Demon Passion ~ We Are Legion by Allison Shepherd

HAIKU SHOTS

*Screaming Banshee ~ Haiku by Darkling
*Manticore Poison ~ Haiku by JE Mason
*Sea-Dragon ~ Haiku by Sarah Yasin
*Vampire Blood ~ Haiku by Diane de Ande
*Sweet Dreams ~ Haiku by Vanessa Noel Graham
*Balloon Poppers ~ Haiku by Minerva Cerridwen
*Dybbuk Possession ~ Haiku by Darkling

PARTY PUNCH

*Tortured Pirate Punch ~ Torture of a Pirate by Ethan Nahté
*Dragon's Claw Punch ~ Food Shopping by Anne M Gibson
*Smokin' Zombie Punch ~ Smoke-town Zombies by James Quinn
*Green Goblin Punch ~ Just Put Out Your Hand by Juleigh Howard-Hobson
*Vampire Champagne Punch ~ Hunger for Life by Andrew Leon Hudson
*Goddess Blackberry Rum Punch ~ My Parent's Don't Like Kali 'Cause She
    Drives a Mustang by Wolf Boy
*Cannabalistic Bourbon Punch ~ Dinner with Jerry by Sally Max
Violet Vampiress Punch ~ Eventide by KA Opperman

Dancing Revenant Punch ~ Sodium-Vapor by Lisa Treece
Sasquatch Mocha Punch ~ When Monsters Share by Shawn Chang
Deadly Sunset Punch ~ Underneath the Red Moon by Linda M Crate
Enchanted Forest Punch ~ Siren of the Woods by Qurat Dar
Tommy's Tappin' Graveyard Punch ~ Tommy's Knocking by Patrick Winters
Deadman's Swamp Punch ~ New Fur for Old Skin by Oliver Smith

BONUS CLOWN SECTION

Clown Night by LS Reinholt
Friend or FOEccacia Bread Sticks
Chocolate Cherry Killer Clown Shake
Colorful Clown Smoothie
Deceptively Sweet Clown Tea
Red Harlequin Party Punch
Balloon Popping Cinnamon Marshmallow Coffee
Evil Jester Cheesecake
Within the Darkness of the Carnivale by Donald Armfield

www.ingramcontent.com/pod-product-compliance
Lightning Source LLC
Chambersburg PA
CBHW040246100426
42811CB00011B/1169